WORKBOOK

Illustration   Fall 2012

Publisher/Owner	>	**BILL DANIELS**
Advertising Sales Director	>	**SUZANNE SEMNACHER**
Advertising Sales	>	**LINDA LEVY** **BOB PASTORE**
Design Director	>	**ANITA ATENCIO**
Director of Production	>	**PAUL SEMNACHER**
Online Portfolio Manager	>	**KIRSTEN LARSON**
Social Media Manager	>	**WILL DANIELS**
Directory Manager	>	**ANGELICA VINTHER**
Directory Marketing Manager	>	**JOHN NIXON**
Directory Verifiers	>	**AURELIO FARRELL II** **JORDAN LACEY** **DAVID PAVAO** **ANGELA PERKINS**
Technology	>	**JIM HUDAK** **STEPHEN CHIANG** **RYAN ADLAF**
Finance	>	**ALLAN GALLANT** **EDUARDO CHEVEZ**
Security	>	**MR. "T"**

connect with

WORKBOOK

B L O G
iPhone
twitter
facebook
linkedin

> Contents

> Index

> Index

*Artist's Representative

> Index

*Artist's Representative

*Artist's Representative

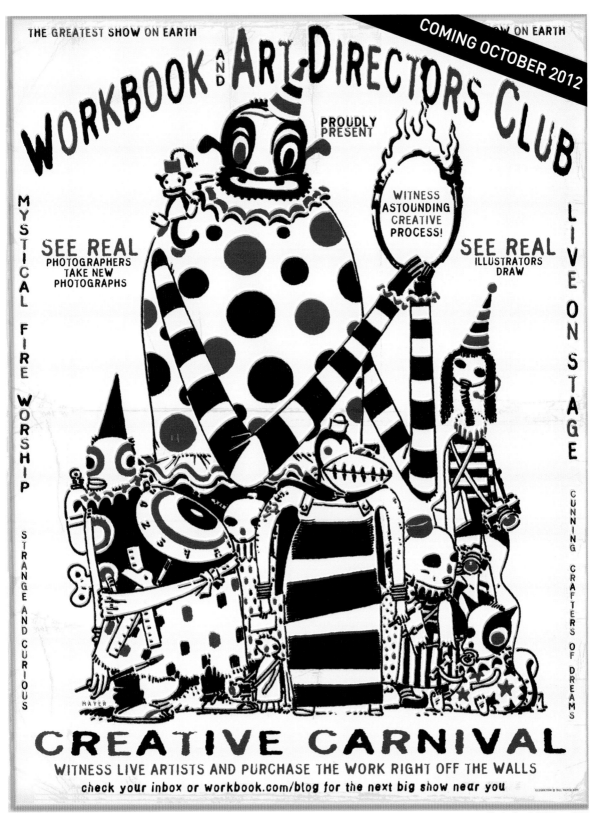

Lettering > Logos > Design

Matt Graif 417.861.8983

MY WAY

Portrait icon of Paul Sr., star of the Discovery Channel's hit show American Chopper.

Matt Graif

Conceptual Icons }

17
361
983

matt@mattgraif.com

1

2

3

4

5

6

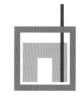

8

7

9

10

11

12

1 Breakfast Bar, 2 Triplets–Birth Announcement, 3 Universal Pictures Movie Title, 4 Apple Infused Moonshine, 5 The Cats–Musical Group, 6 Victorian Beach Front Condo, 7 Heaven and Hell, 8 Nike Paddle Sports, 9 John Deere–Tractor King, 10 Mikayla's Steak House, 11 Andy Williams "Moon River" 75th Anniversary, 12 House Spirits

Mirassou

JOHN STEVENS LETTERING ARTIST & CALLIGRAPHER OF EXPRESSIVE, ILLUSTRATIVE & CLASSIC LETTERFORMS.

I never eat sushi & i have trouble eating things that are merely unconscious

MyDentity

MiniCyn

21 Dog Years
Mike Daisey

Crane Ridge

Mirinda

TWISTER

Ocean

we connect to kids

Me
METABOLIC
EFFECT

BRAVO

WWW.JOHNSTEVENSDESIGN.COM | 336.922.5455

MAGIC KINGDOM

A.1. Steak & Cheese.
It's Back. It's Bold.

La Lupita

move in. Get MORE.

JACK & COKE

the sauce

TOASTMASTER

PACIFIC PLUNGE

Music

Tan Bodies

the premire public.

Just Imagine The Fun!
Now, More Fun Than Ever.

WOK

DISNEY

FRITO LAY

PEPSI

Grand Cafe

NESTLE

EXPRESS yourself.

PHILLIP MORRIS

TAKE THE CHALLENGE
Advil LIQUI-GELS

711

Get Back WITH BiG Mac

CHEVRON

house

That Darn Cat!

GREATFULL TACO
TACOS THAT ROCK

Michelob Light

TEXACO Country SHOWDOWN

CHEVRON

LOGO DESIGN+LETTERING   312.531.2700 | mstroster@earthlink.net

Dia Calhoun

LETTERING & LOGO DESIGN

Adriane Ruggiero

Alaska Airlines

MEDUSA

Sisters of Glass

Vampire

K I N G
&
R A V E N

Swan Lake

Roméo & Juliette

Charlotte Jane Battles Bedtime

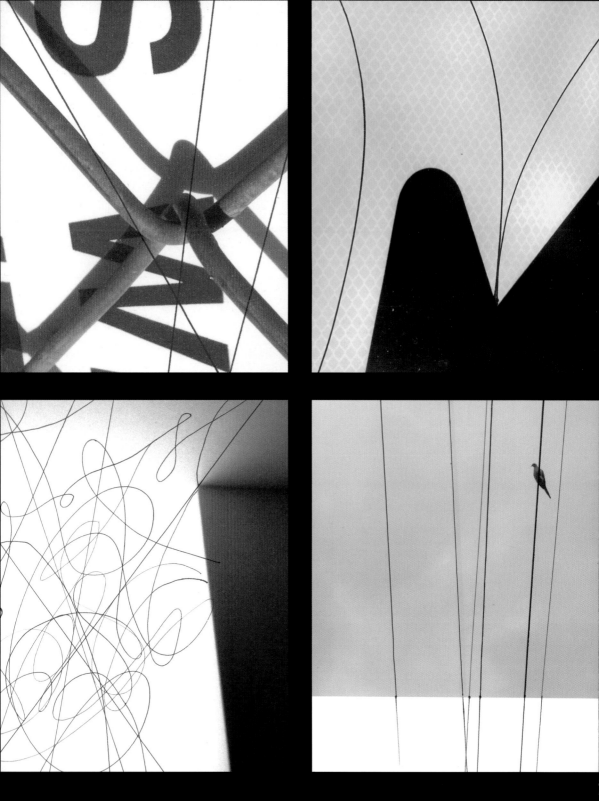

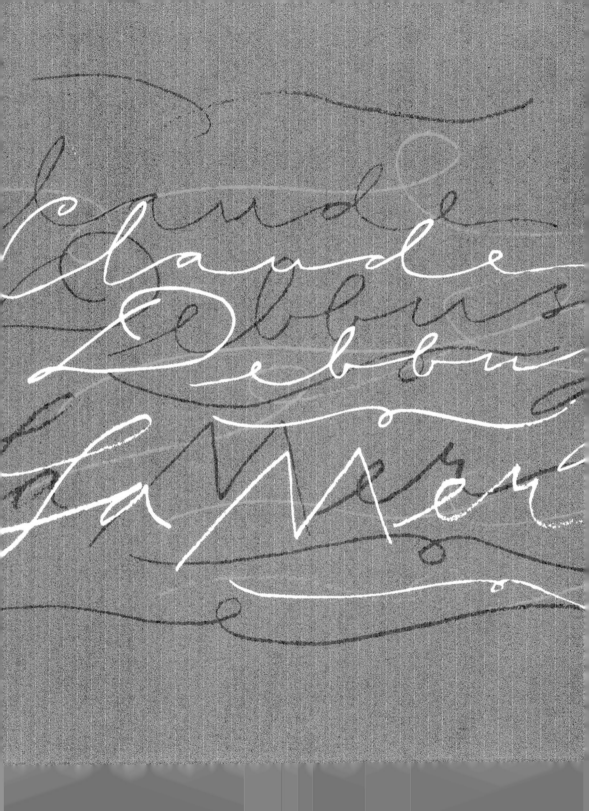

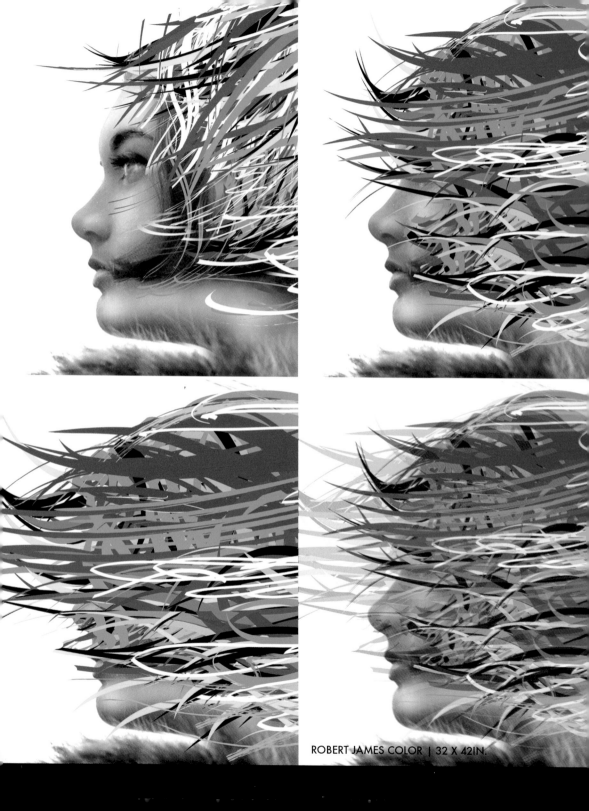

ROBERT JAMES COLOR | 32 X 42IN.

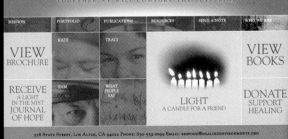

Coravida

Hello, March!

Caraccioli

TAPEO

I Really DIDN'T Say everything I SAID
-Yogi Berra

TAPEO

Tapeo

Tapeo

Little Snugglers

TAPEO

Tapeña

Winery Lake

Madame Woo

OF BEVERLY HILLS

HOTEL

Felix

Ultimate Desserts

Phulay Bay

A RITZ-CARLTON RESERVE

Bolthouse FARMS

D'Alfonso-Curran Wines

hidden pleasures

Luxe Paperie

The Ultimate Stay

Capture Your Hart

PHOTOGRAPHY

Burma Shave

Starstruck

Jill Bell Brandlettering
www.jillbell.com

913.649.4505
jill@jillbell.com

Splendiferous original lettering, logos,
icons, typeface design and modification.

27

Secret
P & G

T TO SAUNTER

FUSIONARY
FUSIONARY TRADING

Performance
OAKLEY

r beautiful option.
KOTEX

ALLING WATER

? It's me, Jackie.
BAYER

B
MAGAZINE

Pampers®
P & G

or, loves glam ROCK.
CLAIROL

INFORMATION DESIGN
THAT MAKES THE
COMPLEX CLEAR

608 828 0280

FUNNEL
INCORPORATED

FUNNELINC.COM

INFOGRAPHICS | INSTRUCTIO
DATA VISUALIZATION | MAPS
CHARTS & GRAPHS | ICONS

Campus map | Client: Minneapolis Institute of Arts

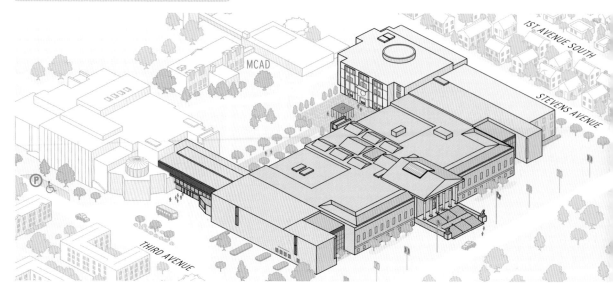

Gallery map detail | Client: Minneapolis Institute of Arts

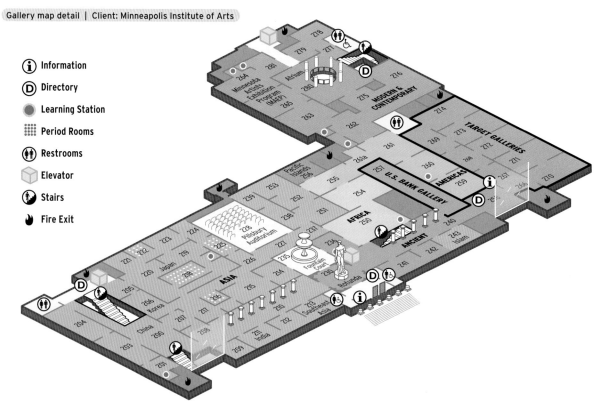

(i) Information

(D) Directory

● Learning Station

▦ Period Rooms

(♀♂) Restrooms

⬜ Elevator

(👤) Stairs

🔥 Fire Exit

INFORMATION DESIGN
THAT MAKES THE
COMPLEX CLEAR

608 828 0280

FUNNEL
INCORPORATED

FUNNELINC.COM

INFOGRAPHICS | INSTRUCTIONS
DATA VISUALIZATION | MAPS
CHARTS & GRAPHS | ICONS

Las Vegas map elements | Client: R&R Partners | Brand: Las Vegas Convention and Visitors Authority

LUXOR
EXCALIBUR
TROPICANA
NEW YORK NEW YORK
MGM GRAND
MONTE CARLO
VDARA
ARIA
THE COSMOPOLITAN
PARIS

Product icons | Client: Aprilaire

Humidifier   Air Cleaner   Dehumidifier   Ventilation   Zone Comfort Control   UV Light   Thermostat

Icons for online game | Client: DDB | Brand: Clorox

Various Icons

Interactive infographic elements | Client: 22 Squared | Brand: Toyota

TRACTION

TRACTION

Instruction design for bike computer | Client: Saris CycleOps

STEM MOUNT

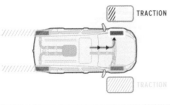

Rings: Crisscross under
em, latch on hooks

OR

Zip tie around stem,
through slots

BATTERY

3 Volt
#CR2032

INTERVAL & RIDE MODE

Press & Hold
3 sec. to go
back to Ride
Mode

INTERVAL 1
INTERVAL 2

UP TO 99 INTERVALS

DASHBOARD 1

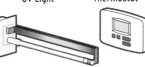

• 1x

Press 1x

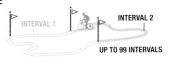

11:31 A   432   Current Power
Watts
Distance
123.5   25.3   + 1x
Avg/Max Bar Graph   Max Watts
Avg Watts   194   597

11:31 A   432   Current Speed
123.5   25.3   + 1x
Avg Speed   Max Speed
17.8   32.5

11:31 A   432
Ride distance
123.5   25.3   Ride Time
KJ   RIDE
849   1:23:31
Work

AUGUSTA
PLASTIC SURGERY

Sabor Casero

w FERNANDEZSTUDIO.COM   e CARLOS@FERNANDEZSTUDIO.COM   t 512.619.4020

BOLD

sensational

now

hurry

MAGIC

Quick

easy

Amazing

Sandra Bruce

LETTERING & ILLUSTRATION (530) 477-1909 WWW.SANDRABRUCE.COM

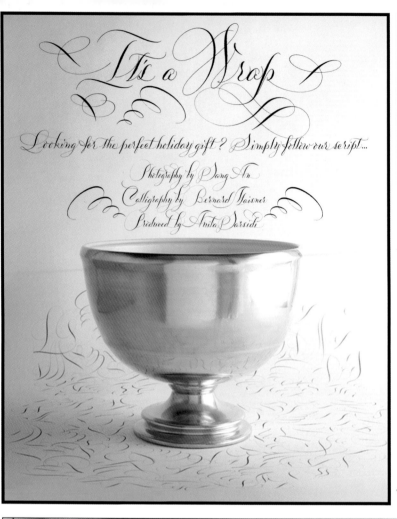

It's a Wrap

Looking for the perfect holiday gift? Simply follow our script...

Photography by Sang An

Calligraphy by Bernard Maisner

Produced by Anita Sarsidi

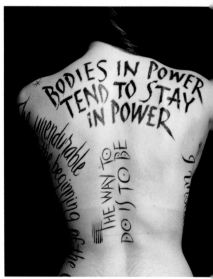

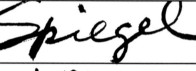

BERNARD MAISNER
HAND-LETTERING

PRESENTED BY GERALD & CULLEN RAPP
212-889-3337
W.RAPPART.COM INFO@RAPPART.COM

BO JACKSON'S
SWEET POTATO
FRESH · FLAKEY
PIE
FLOUR

Orville

THE
ULTIMATE
TAILGATE PARTY
RULE THE LOT

HARLEY DAVIDSON · HARLEY-DAVIDSON MOTOR CYCLES · 2010 VRSC V-ROD

The Original
·SOUPMAN

Twizzlers
Strawberry TWISTS

A

ISKRA DESIGN

If you've been wondering if the like button is the only way to express your affection, there ARE alternatives.......

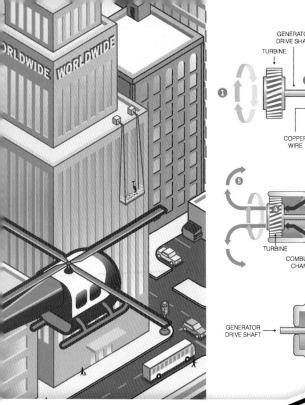

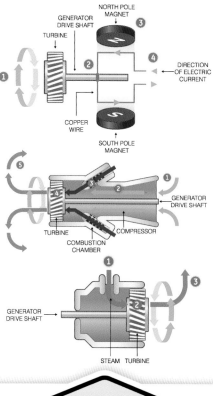

GENERATOR DRIVE SHAFT

TURBINE

NORTH POLE MAGNET

1 **2** **3** **4**

DIRECTION OF ELECTRIC CURRENT

COPPER WIRE

SOUTH POLE MAGNET

5 **3** **1** **2** **4**

GENERATOR DRIVE SHAFT

TURBINE **COMBUSTION CHAMBER** **COMPRESSOR**

1 **2** **3**

GENERATOR DRIVE SHAFT

STEAM **TURBINE**

1 To walk on ice, keep your center of gra[vity] over your front leg.

2 One animal that has figured this out is [the] penguin. Think of yourself as a pengui[n] and you'll be all right.

1 **2**

HOW TO WALK ON ICE

TABLETINFOGRAPHICS.COM

TABLET
INFOGRAPHICS

608.692.1629

> Illustration

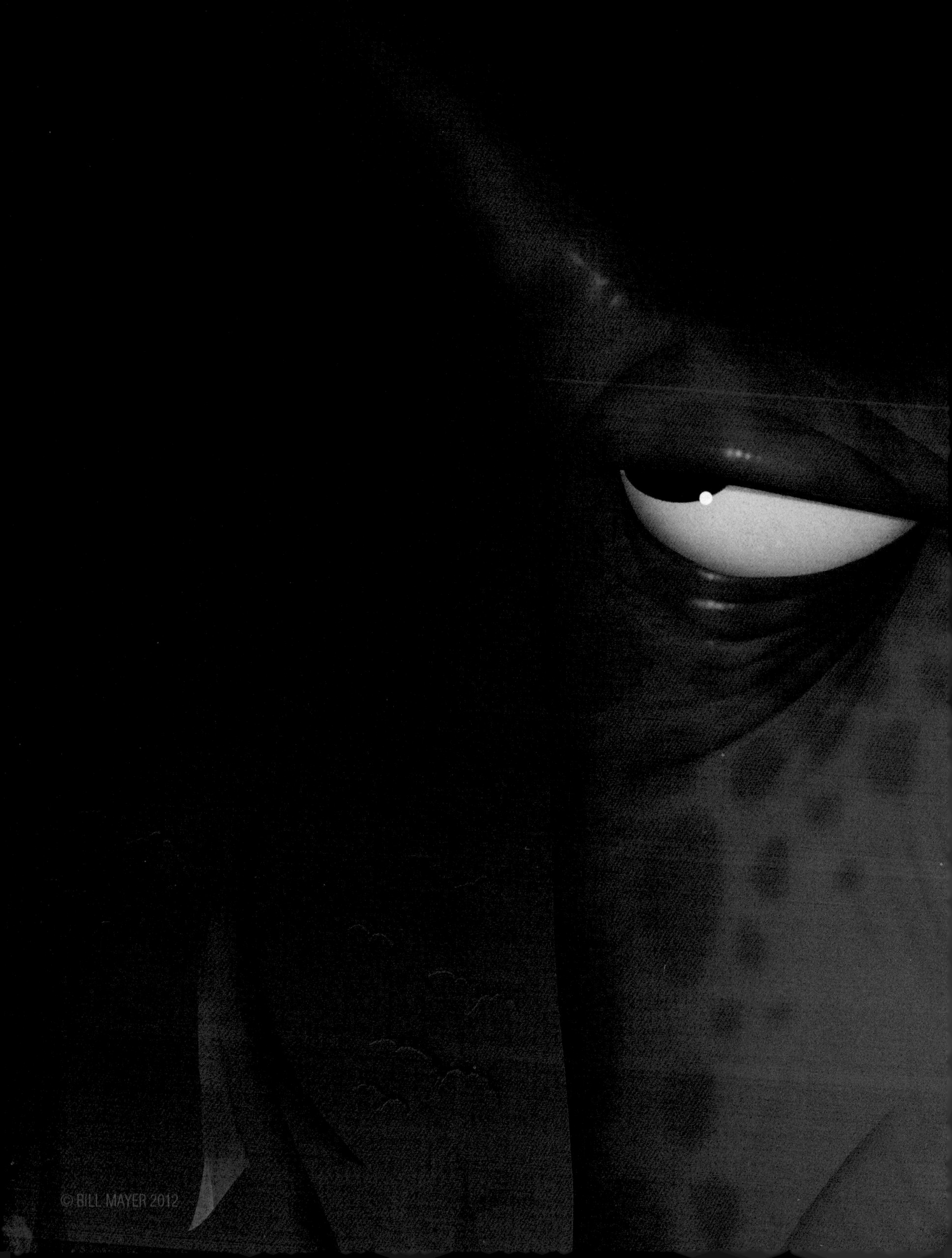

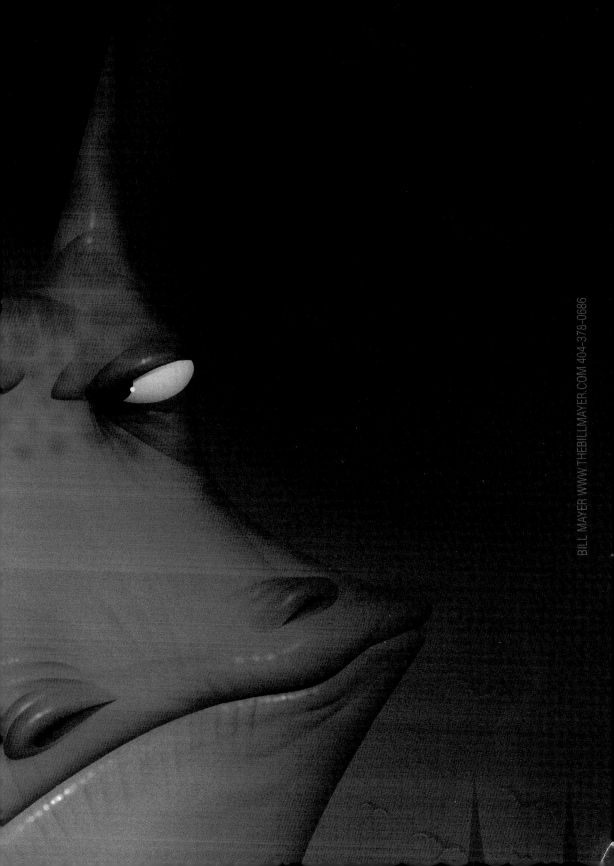

JOHN BURGOYNE

Yellow Brandywine

Flammé

Moskvich

Green Zebra

Wonder Light

Debarao

German

Valencia

Cherokee Purple

Nepal

Great White Beefsteak

HEIRLOOM TOMATOES

STUDIO 508.362.9236
WWW.JOHNBURGOYNE.COM

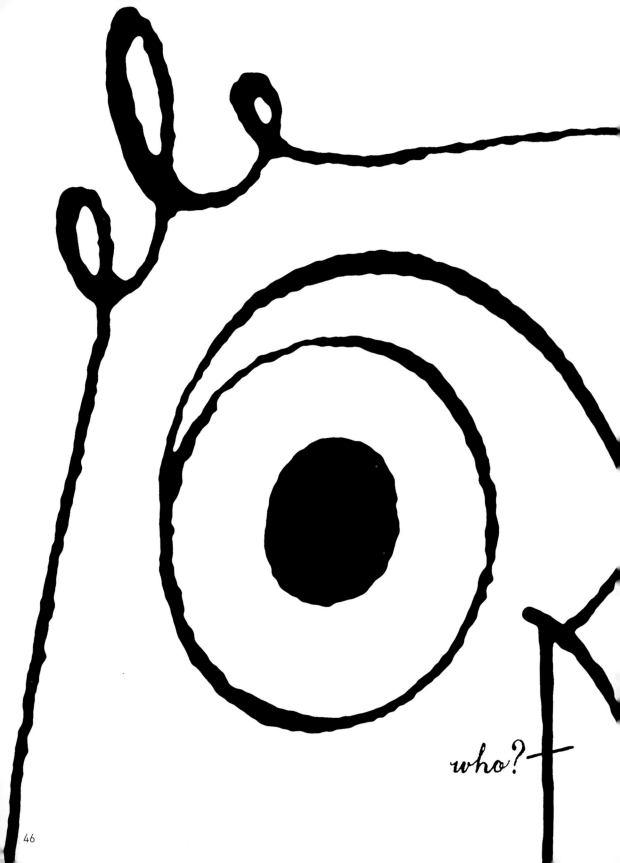

who?

Elvis Swift

EST SIDE STORY

The
Barber
of
Seville

Steve Bjorkman

949-349-0109
stevebjorkman.com
stevebjorkman@sbcglobal.net

Jeff Koegel / koegeldesign.com / 949-463-2576

Rome

Veronica Lawlor
illustration

veronica@studio1482.com

917-449-9425

1482

studio 1482

A&K Luxury Travel

Dr. Don Francis, CEO

reportage drawings for VaxGen annual report

Barbara Tyler

fashionillustrationandmore.com
Lott Representatives • 212 • 755 • 5737
lottreps.com

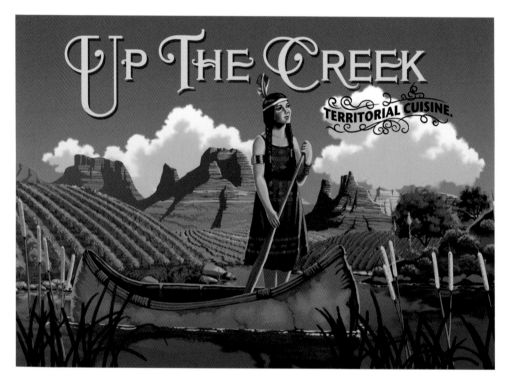

HEDGE
ARTIST REPRESENTATIVE

BONNIE HOFKIN

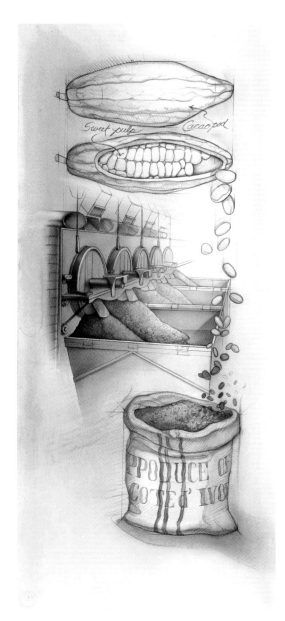

WWW.HOFKIN.HEDGEREPS.COM

WWW.HEDGEREPS.COM

818·244·0110
JOANNE@HEDGEREPS.COM

MOBILE
SCAN
LINK

57

TOM LYNCH
Drawings for stories and ideas.

718.494.0118 TOM@HAVOCMEDIA.COM

WWW.WentSketching.BLOGSPOT.COM

WWW.HAVOCMEDIA.COM

HAVOC
MEDIA DESIGN

Robert Neubecker
Gerald & Cullen Rapp
212 889 3337
info@rappart.com
www.rappart.com/ neubecker.com

Gerald & Cullen Rapp

212-889-3337
info@rappart.com
www.rappart.com

EVA VÁZQUEZ evavazquezdibujos.com

ASAF HANUKA

Gerald & Cullen Rapp   212.889.3337   info@rappart.com   www.rappart.com

 dh daniel hertzberg illustration

Represented by Gerald & Cullen Rapp

(212) 889-3337 | info@rappart.com

www.danielhertzberg.com | www.rappart.com

YUTA ONODA
www.yutaonoda.com

Gerald & Cullen Rapp | 212.899.3337
info@rappart.com | www.rappart.com

GILL LEWIS

WILD WINGS

H A N K O S U N A
Represented by Gerald & Cullen Rapp
212.889.3337

INFO@RAPPART.COM
WWW.RAPPART.COM
WWW.HANKOSUNA.COM

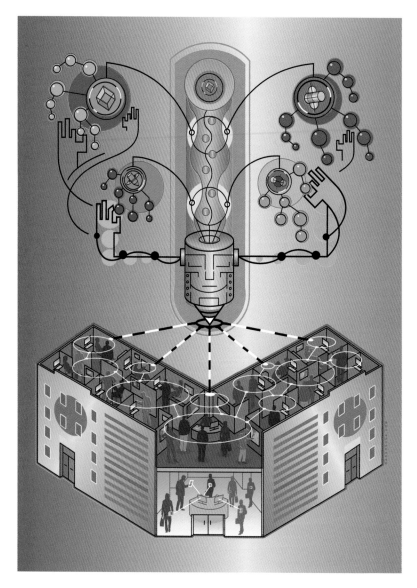

Gerald & Cullen Rapp
212 889 3337
info@rappart.com
www.rappart.com
www.elizabethtraynor.com

ELIZABETH TRAYNOR

Watercolor
&
Scratchboard

Phil Wrigglesworth
GERALD+CULLEN RAPP
• 212-889-8337 •
info@rappart.com
www.rappart.com

JON REINFURT

+ GERALD AND CULLEN RAPP
+ 212 889 3337
+ WWW.RAPPART.COM
+ INFO@RAPPART.COM

David M. Brinley
Gerald & Cullen Rapp
212.889.3337
info@rappart.com
www.rappart.com
www.davidbrinley.com

NIGEL BUCHANAN Represented by Gerald and Cullen Rapp
212.889.3337 info@rappart.com **www.rappart.com** www.nigelbuchanan.com

Lonnie Busch
represented by Gerald & Cullen Rapp

212-889-3337
info@rappart.com
www.rappart.com
www.lonniebusch.com

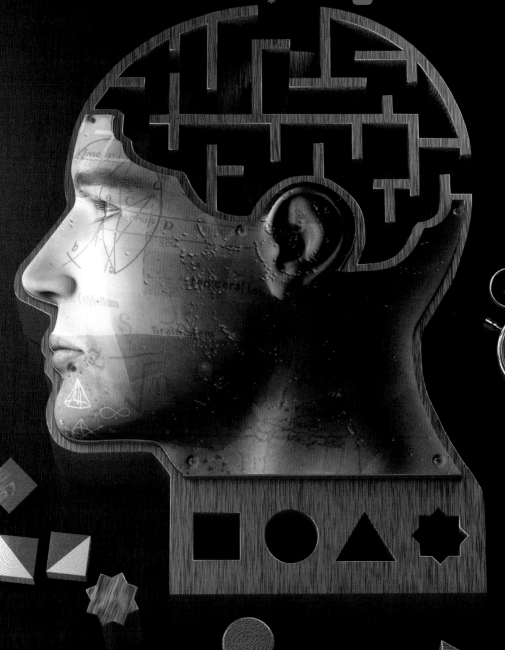

Daniel Keyes
Flowers for Algernon

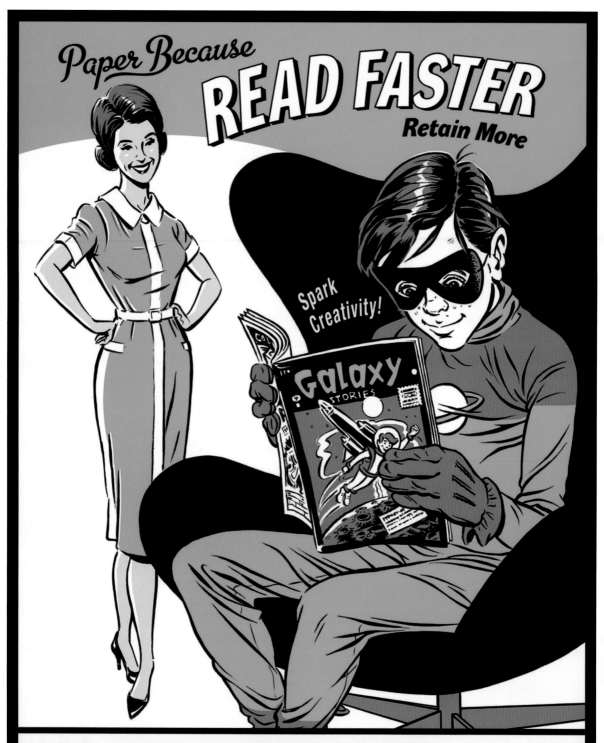

Inside every reader is a Super Reader! To find your hidden powers, simply read on paper. Studies show you'll read up to 30% faster while retaining more information. You'll fly through sentences faster than a space rocket. Impress your family and friends today! Learn more at paperbecause.com.

Jonathan Carlson

Gerald & Cullen Rapp
212-889-3337
www.rappart.com
info@rappart.com

WALL ST

Business Mian

STEPHANIE DALTON COWAN

Gerald & Cullen Rapp   212.889.3337

www.rappart.com   info@rappart.com

www.daltoncowan.com

Austin Lyric Opera: The Marriage of Figaro

Austin Lyric Opera: Faust

Jan Feindt

represented by
Gerald & Cullen Rapp
212.889.3337 | janfeindt.de
rappart.com | info@rappart.com

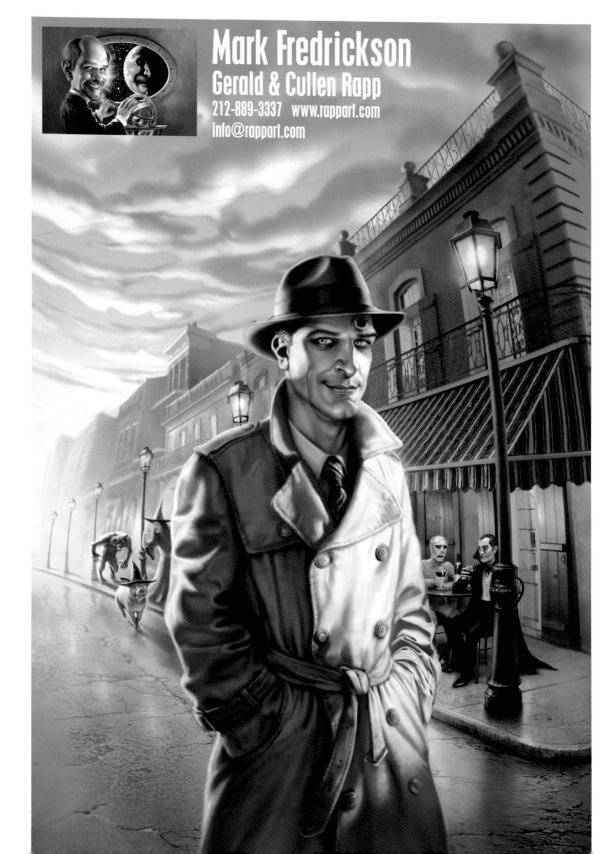

Mark Fredrickson
Gerald & Cullen Rapp
212-889-3337   www.rappart.com
info@rappart.com

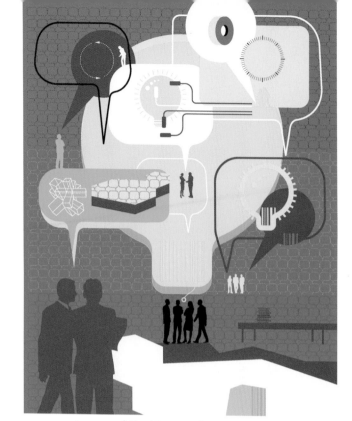

www.rappart.com/Celia_Johnson

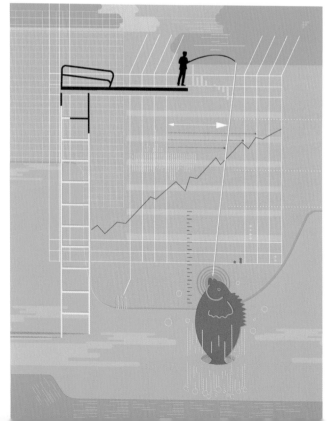

CELIA JOHNSON

GERALD & CULLEN RAPP
212 889 3337

info@rappart.com
www.rappart.com

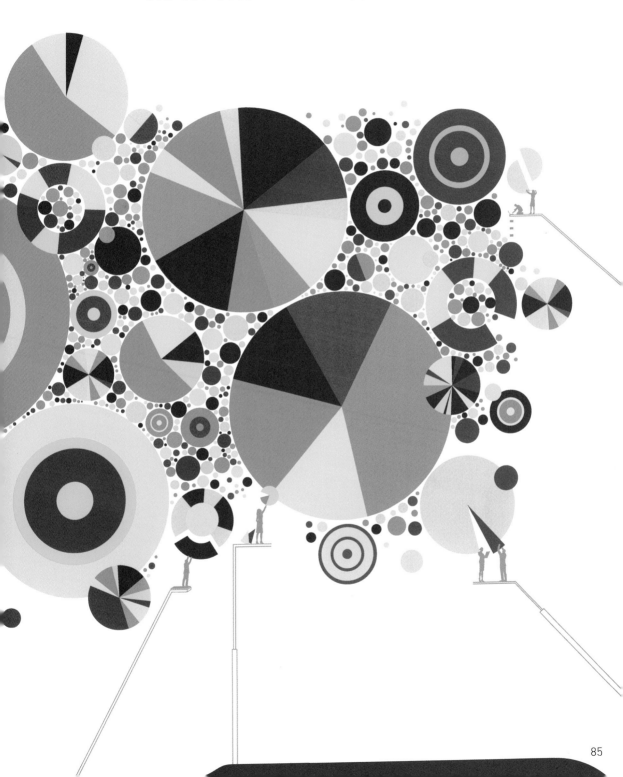

Laszlo Kubinyi

Gerald & Cullen Rapp

212 889 3337
info@rappart.com
www.rappart.com

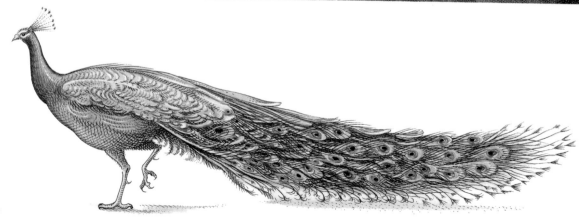

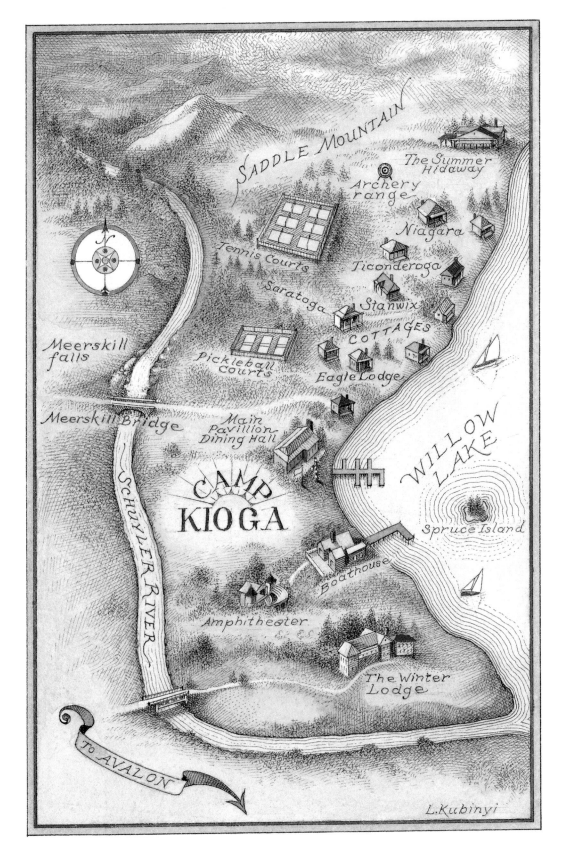

Sean McCabe

GERALD & CULLEN RAPP
212.889 3337 / info@rappart.com
www.rappart.com / www.wider-than-pictures.com

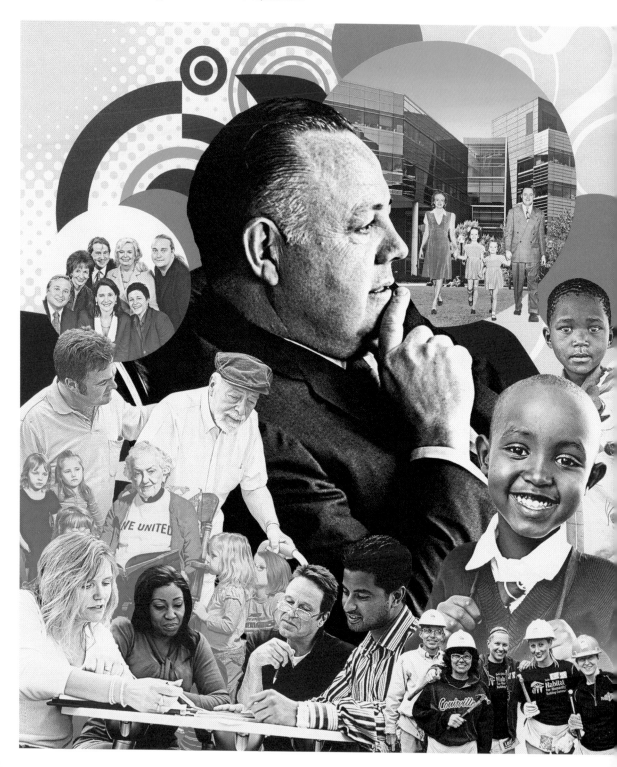

Richard Mia

Gerald & Cullen Rapp
212–889–3337
info@rappart.com
www.rappart.com

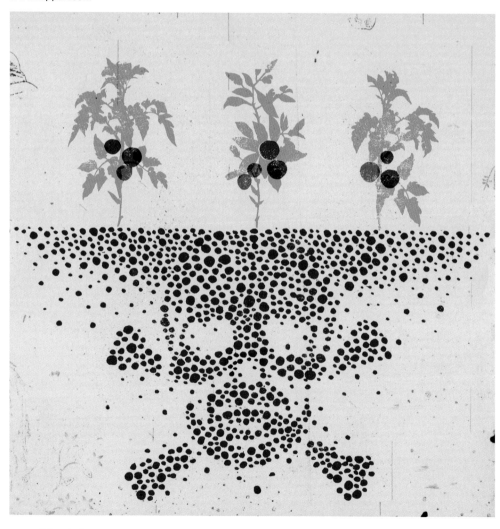

www.richardmia.com

Bruce Morser

Gerald & Cullen Rapp
212 889 3337
info@rappart.com
www.rappart.com

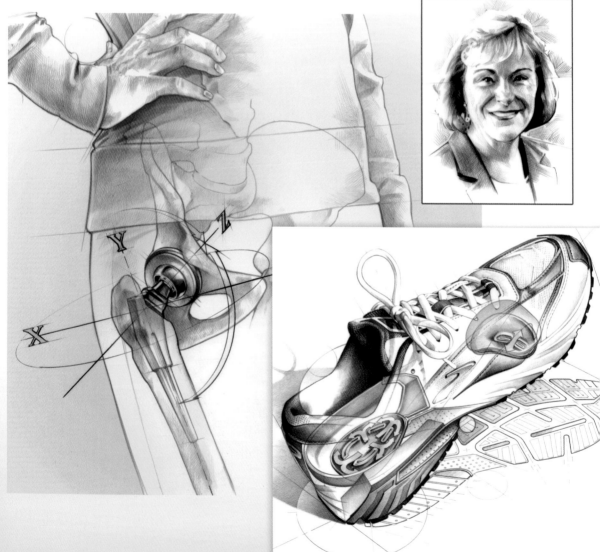

CAPTURING and REUSING ENERGY

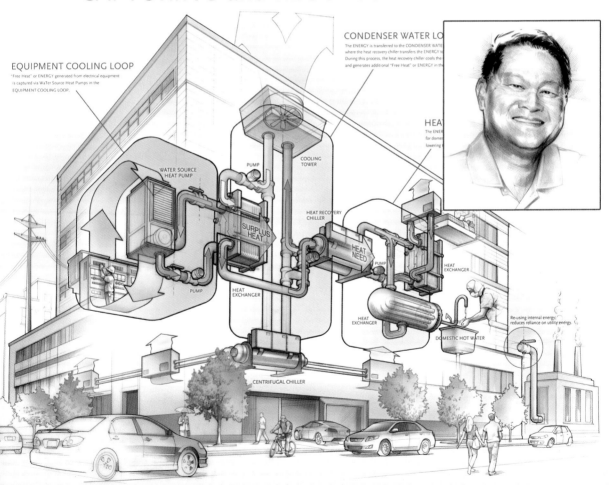

EQUIPMENT COOLING LOOP
"Free Heat" or ENERGY generated from electrical equipment
is captured via WaTer Source Heat Pumps in the
EQUIPMENT COOLING LOOP.

CONDENSER WATER LO
The ENERGY is transferred to the CONDENSER WATE
where the heat recovery chiller transfers the ENERGY to
During this process, the heat recovery chiller cools the
and generates additional "Free Heat" or ENERGY in the

HEA
The ENER
for dome
lowering

WATER SOURCE
HEAT PUMP

PUMP

COOLING
TOWER

SURPLUS
HEAT

HEAT RECOVERY
CHILLER

HEAT
NEED

PUMP

HEAT
EXCHANGER

PUMP

HEAT
EXCHANGER

Re-using internal energy,
reduces reliance on utility energy.

HEAT
EXCHANGER

DOMESTIC HOT WATER

CENTRIFUGAL CHILLER

Floyd & Delores Jones Pavilion at Virginia Mason Medical Center
EnviroMason's commitment to energy efficiency

the GREAT Outdoors

Shaw Nielsen
SHAWNIELSEN.COM

GERALD & CULLEN RAPP
WWW.RAPPART.COM
INFO@RAPPART.COM
212-889-3337

95

Dan Page

Gerald & Cullen Rapp | 212-889-3337 | info@rappart.com | www.rappart.com

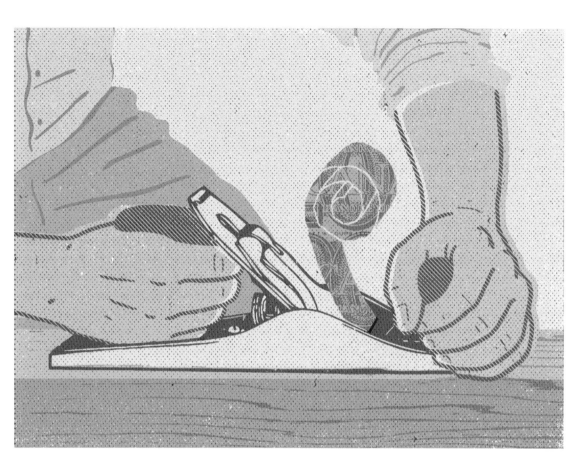

MARC ROSENTHAL REPRESENTED BY GERALD& CULLEN RAPP
212-889-3337 • INFO@RAPPART.COM
WWW.RAPPART.COM • WWW.MARC-ROSENTHAL.COM

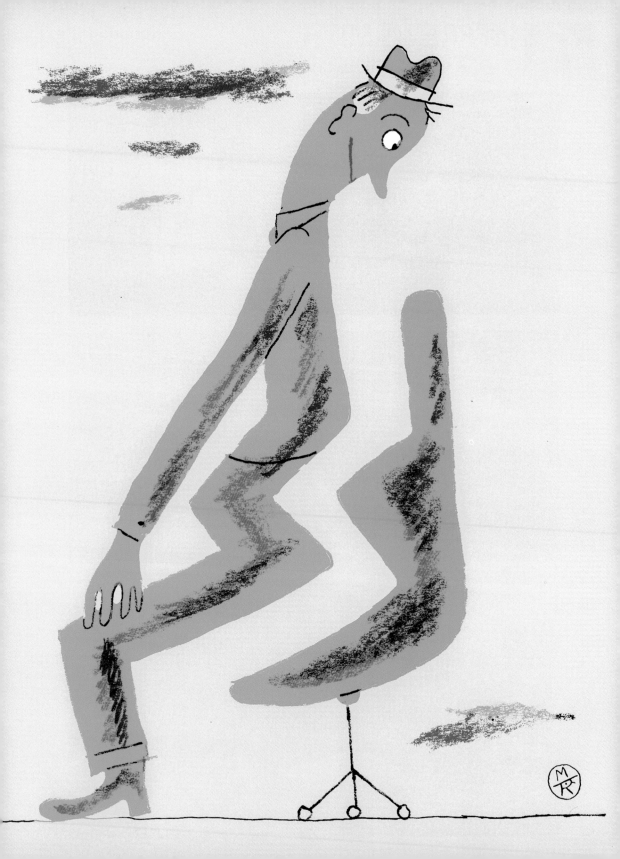

RYAN SNOOK

Represented by
Gerald & Cullen Rapp

212-889-3337
info@rappart.com
www.rappart.com

ryansnook.com
twitter.com/ryansnook

Bengal Tiger
panthera tigris tigris

BENGAL TIGER

The Bengal Tiger, panthera tigris tigris, or Indian tiger is the most numerous of the 5 remaining tiger subspecies. 3 tiger subspecies were made extinct in the 20th century and those remaining are classified as endangered. The Bengal is recognized by it's yellow to light orange coat and dark brown to black stripes. A fierce nocturnal hunter, it may consume up to 60 pounds of Buffalo, Deer, Wild Pigs, or other mammals in one night.

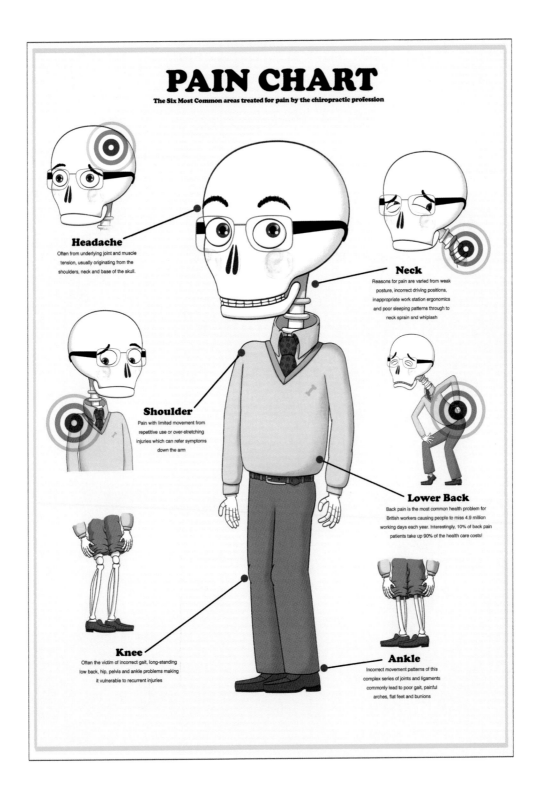

PAIN CHART

The Six Most Common areas treated for pain by the chiropractic profession

Headache
Often from underlying joint and muscle tension, usually originating from the shoulders, neck and base of the skull.

Neck
Reasons for pain are varied from weak posture, incorrect driving positions, inappropriate work station ergonomics and poor sleeping patterns through to neck sprain and whiplash

Shoulder
Pain with limited movement from repetitive use or over-stretching injuries which can refer symptoms down the arm

Lower Back
Back pain is the most common health problem for British workers causing people to miss 4.9 million working days each year. Interestingly, 10% of back pain patients take up 90% of the health care costs!

Knee
Often the victim of incorrect gait, long-standing low back, hip, pelvis and ankle problems making it vulnerable to recurrent injuries

Ankle
Incorrect movement patterns of this complex series of joints and ligaments commonly lead to poor gait, painful arches, flat feet and bunions

Michael Witte

Gerald & Cullen Rapp

212 889 3337
info@rappart.com
www.rappart.com

Noah Woods

Gerald & Cullen Rapp
212-889-3337

www.noahwoods.com
info@rappart.com
www.rappart.com

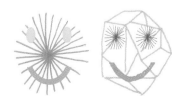

JAMES O'BRIEN

Brian Ajhar

Gerald & Cullen Rapp

212 889 3337
info@rappart.com
www.rappart.com

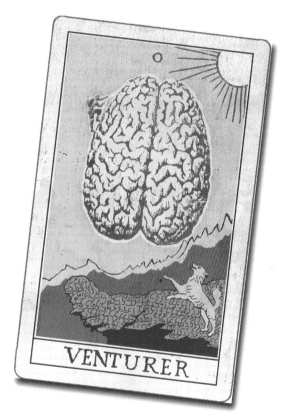

VENTURER

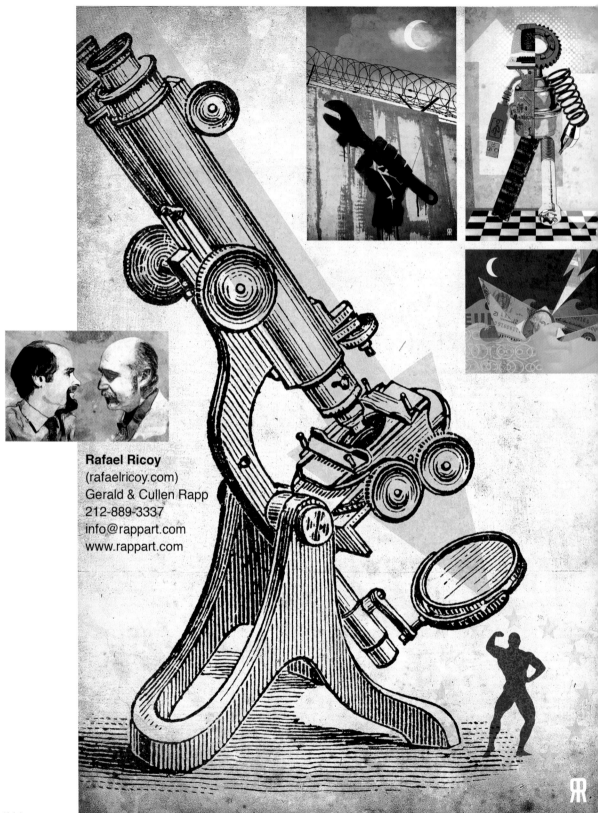

Rafael Ricoy
(rafaelricoy.com)
Gerald & Cullen Rapp
212-889-3337
info@rappart.com
www.rappart.com

COTTY REIFSNYDER

Gerald & Cullen Rapp
212.889.3337
www.rappart.com
info@rappart.com

James Steinberg

Gerald & Cullen Rapp | 212-889-3337 | info@rappart.com
www.james-steinberg.com | www.rappart.com

"Retail is the business I'm in, but that doesn't sound personal enough to me. So I like to think of myself as a shopkeeper in the village of my neighborhood." ~ Phoebe Cates, FOUNDER, Blue Tree.
(pls. see p.24)

JOHN S. DYKES
ILLUSTRATION

www.JSDYKES.com   www.RAPPART.com
info@RAPPART.com   212.889.3337
GERALD & CULLEN RAPP

anders wenngren • gerald & cullen rapp • 212 889-3337 • info@rappart.com • www.rappart.com

JAKOB HINRICHS

Neal Aspinall

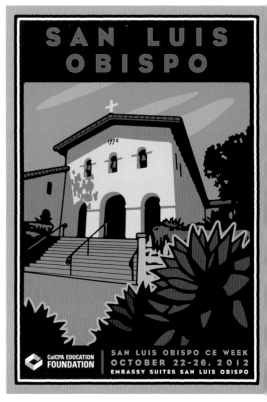

Tim O'Brien ~ **obrienillustration.com**

(718) 282-2821 ~ obrienillustration@me.com ~ Agent: Peter Lott ~ (212) 755-5737

LINDA FENNIMORE | LZFENNIMORE@VERIZON.NET

(212) 866 - 0279 | WORKBOOK.COM/PORTFOLIOS/FENNIMORE

Raphael Montoliu   www.montoliustudio.com   raphael@konocti.net   707 263 6143

SEATTLE MAGAZINE

QUIRK BOO

TOMMY HILFIGER

KOKANEE BEER

LARRY JOST

Represented by Susan and Co. • 206 232 7873 • www.susanandco.com • www.larryjostillustration.com

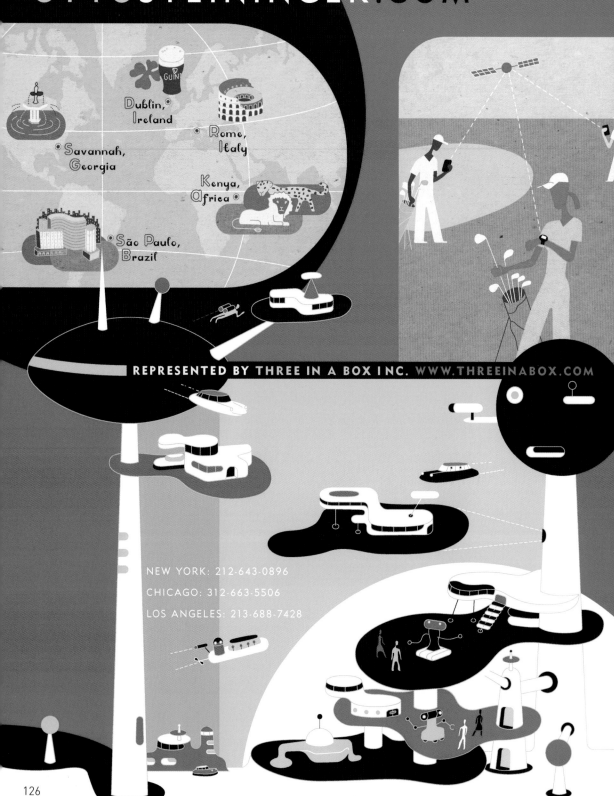

OTTOSTEININGER.COM

Dublin, Ireland

GUINN

Rome, Italy

Savannah, Georgia

Kenya, Africa

São Paulo, Brazil

REPRESENTED BY THREE IN A BOX INC. WWW.THREEINABOX.COM

NEW YORK: 212-643-0896

CHICAGO: 312-663-5506

LOS ANGELES: 213-688-7428

tom hennessy • www.hennessyart.com • tom@hennessyart.com • Tel: 707 559 5341
www.workbook.com/portfolios/hennessy

VALENTINA BELLONI

MELA BOLINAO T 212 689.7830 F 212 689.7829 www.mbartists.com

MB artists

MELA BOLINAO T 212 689.7830 F 212 689.7829 www.mbartists.com

     MELA BOLINAO **T** 212 689.7830 **F** 212 689.7829 www.mbartists.com

MIKE REED

MELA BOLINAO T 212 689.7830 F 212 689.7829 www.mbartists.com

HECTOR BORLASCA

LINDA BRONSON

VALERIA CIS

SERGIO DE GIORGI

MELA BOLINAO T 212 689.7830 F 212 689.7829 www.mbartists.com

ELDON DOTY

CAROLINA FARÍAS

MELA BOLINAO   T 212 689.7830   F 212 689.7829   www.mbartists.com

JANNIE HO

LAURA HULISKA-BEITH

MELA BOLINAO   T 212 689.7830   F 212 689.7829   www.mbartists.com

HIROE NAKATA

MACKY PAMINTUAN

ildren's Entertainment: Backstory, Character & Product Development & Design for Hasbro, Mattel, CBS

ade Books: Abrams, Simon & Schuster, Lyons & Burford, National Geographic Books, Abbeville

ildren's Books: HarperCollins, Zondervan, Little Brown, Knopf, Doubleday, Hyperion, Crown

ommercial: American Express, AT&T, Leupold Optics, Citibank, FedEx, Ford, Time,

ives of Alaska, Adidas, Burger King, Life, Newsweek, Cabela's, Parks Canada,

ty of Chicago, CNN, Turner Broadcasting, Field & Stream, Jarrett Rifles

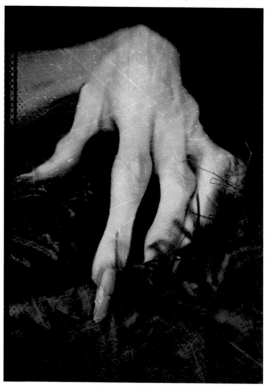

Neil Brennan

757 · 875 · 0148

neilbrennan.com

PENELOPE DULLAGHAN

REPRESENTED BY SCOTT HULL ASSOCIATES

(937) 433-8383 // SCOTT@SCOTTHULL.COM

SCOTTHULL.COM // PENELOPEDULLAGHAN.COM

© Copyright 2012 - Monkey Inferno - Evolution

© Copyright 2012 Old Mountain Moonshine

© Copyright 2011 The Vermont Country Store

© Copyright 2011 St. George Spirits - Dragon

© Copyright 2011 Ten High

© Copyright 2012 Mill Creek Winery

© Copyright 2011 WesBanco

© Copyright 2012 William Sonoma

© Copyright 2011 Dominos Pizza

SLS

© Copyright 2011 SLS Hotels logo

World Class Illustrations from over 3,500 images and over 1,000 stock illustrations for clients from all over the world!

2006 Rosey Awards • Mead Show Award Winner 2001 • Brand New 2009 • Ad Pulp 2009 • Communications Arts 1997 • National Addy Awards 2010

© Copyright 2012 Got Milk

© Copyright 2012 Short Mountain Shine

© 2012 American Express

AMERICAN EXPRESS

© Copyright 2011 La Tortilla Factory

© Copyright 2012 Zaro's Bakery

© Copyright 2012 Medjool Dates

Est. 1879

© Copyright 2011 Inglenook Vineyards

World Class Illustrations from over 3,500 images and over 1,000 stock illustrations for clients from all over the world!

© Copyright 2011 William Sonoma

© Copyright 2012 Kraken Rum

© Copyright 2011 Noble Illustrations

© Copyright 2011 Healthy Choice

MT. TAM

© Copyright 2012 St. George Spirits

© Copyright 2012 George School

© Copyright 2011 Manor Hall

© Copyright 2012 Fetzer Vineyards

• stock images: www.scratchboardstock.net •
World Class Illustrations from over 3,500 images and over 1,000 stock illustrations for clients from all over the world!

2006 Rosey Awards • Mead Show Award Winner 2001 • Brand New 2009 • Ad Pulp 2009 • Communications Arts 1997 • National Addy Awards 2010

Roger Xavier
SCRATCHBOARD LINE ILLUSTRATIONS

GLUTEN FREE
CRUST

BRAN

MUNROCAMPAGNA.COM
E. steve@munrocampagna.com   P. 312.335.8925
630 N State St #2109 Chicago, IL 60654

Anne Wertheim

MUNRO
CAMPAGNA
ARTIST
REPRESENTATIVES

Mike Kasun

MUNROCAMPAGNA.COM
E. steve@munrocampagna.com   P. 312.335.8925
630 N State St #2109 Chicago, IL 60654

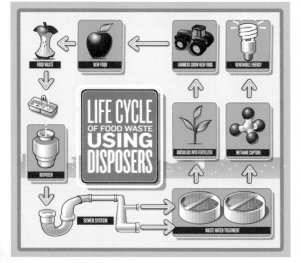

MUNROCAMPAGNA.COM
E. steve@munrocampagna.com   P. 312.335.8925
630 N State St #2109 Chicago, IL 60654

MUNRO
CAMPAGNA
ARTIST
REPRESENTATIVES

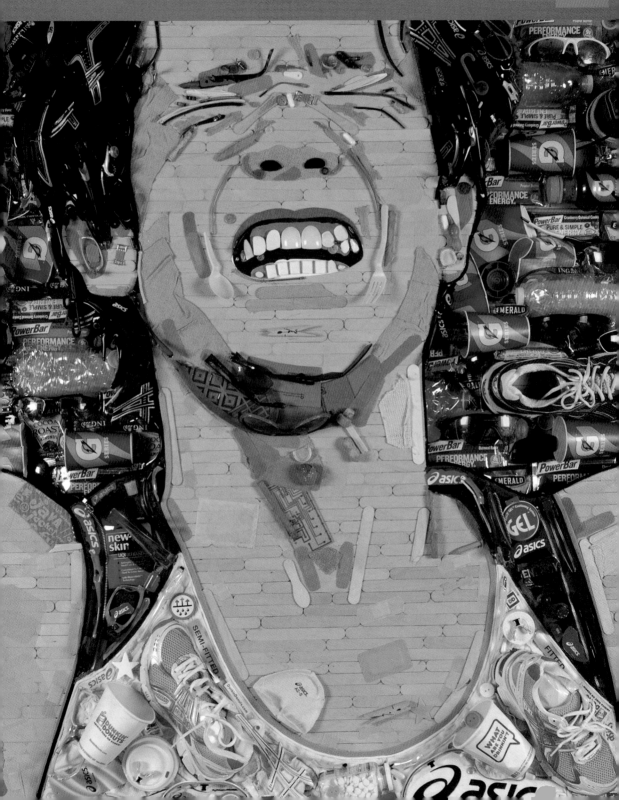

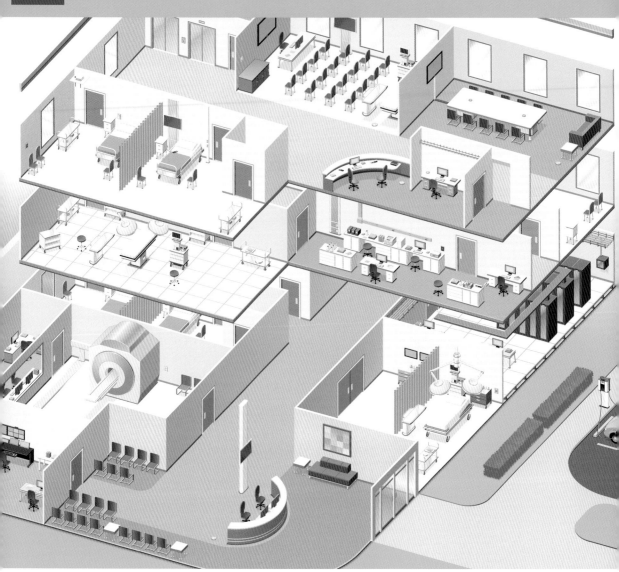

David Preiss

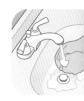

MUNROCAMPAGNA.COM
E. steve@munrocampagna.com   P. 312.335.8925
630 N State St #2109 Chicago, IL 60654

MUNROCAMPAGNA.COM
E. steve@munrocampagna.com   P. 312.335.8925
630 N State St #2109 Chicago, IL 60654

Keith Negley

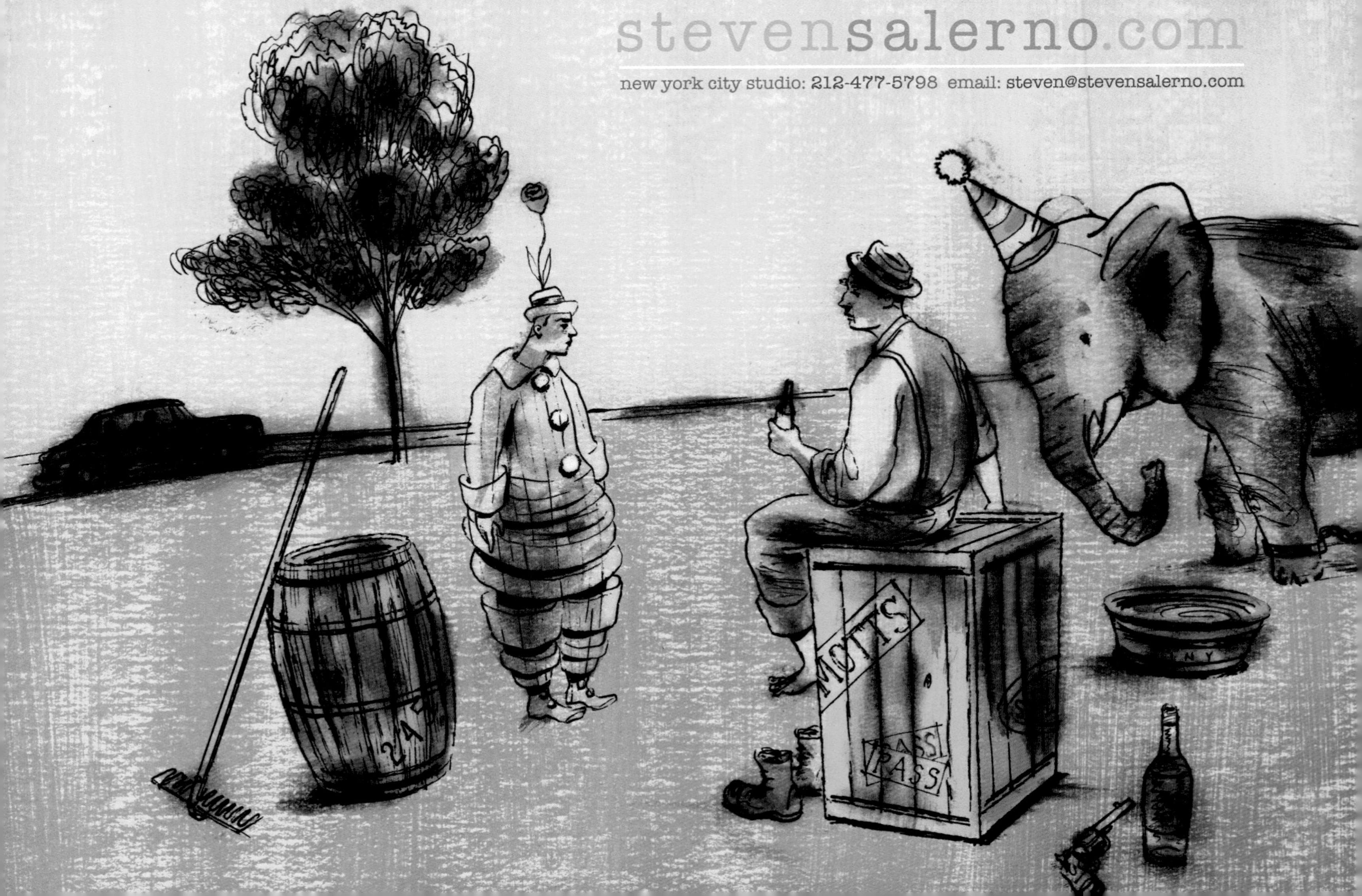
MOTTS
PASS
PASS

Trip Park 704.347.2844 trippark.blogspot.com

Meghann Powell

monica lind

WSW
creative
212 431 4480
wswcreative.com

Midwest: Anne Albrecht
847 881 2572
annealbrecht.com

garylacoste.com

413.967.7446 • gary@garylacoste.com

RICHARD THOMPSON *ILLUSTRATION*

Visual problem solving, digital image creation and photo retouching services. I use Photoshop, 3D software and digital photography to create images for billboards, posters, transit shelters, point of purchase, packaging, magazine, corporate collateral, direct mail and anything else you can think of. With 20 years of experience, my specialty is short deadlines ;-) Visit my website to request a free printed portfolio, to see over 100 images and check out the section on how it's all done:

WWW.RTILLUSTRATION.COM

E-MAIL: RICK@RTILLUSTRATION.COM   PHONE: 1-905-425-0093   CELL: 1-905-718-9633

For the fruitiest High Juice

Illustration

Agents
Stacey Endress Victoria Pearce
Juliette Lott   Mike Cowley

illustrationweb.com   23 Ohio Stre
973.763.1712   Maplewood
howdy@illustrationweb.com   NJ 07040

JUICE
KLICK
◀ IGNITE

REIMAGINE
IMOTIV

illustrationweb.com   howdy@illustrationweb.com   973.763.1712

Illustration

BoomArtwork
Paul Holland

Gail Armstrong
Pete Pachoumis

Alex Fuentes ▶

Miss Led
Nuno DaCosta

Montana Forbes
Christian David Moore

◀ Lucia Emanuela Curzi

illustrationweb.com   howdy@illustrationweb.com   973.763.1712   *Illustration*

Fernando Juarez
Bill Greenhead

T.S Spookytooth
Alexandra Ball

Mark Oliver ▶

 illustrationweb.com   howdy@illustrationweb.com   973.763.1712

Syd Brak
Kathryn Rathke

◀ Philip Bannister

Richard Phipps
Rosie Sanders

illustrationweb.com   howdy@illustrationweb.com   973.763.1712   *Illustration*

cocotos.com

illustration • animation • stock

tom@cocotos.com 212.620.7556

DON SIPLEY

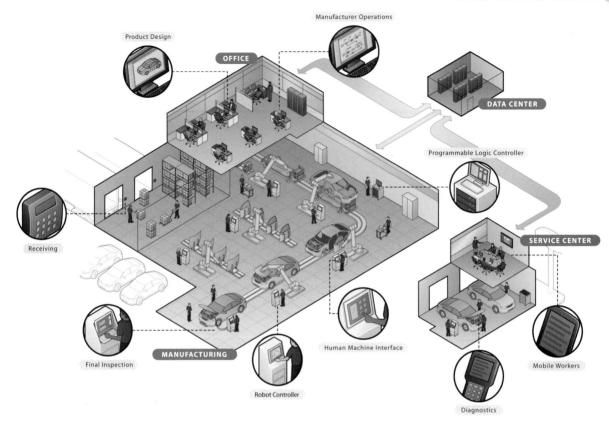

TOPDOG™
ILLUSTRATION

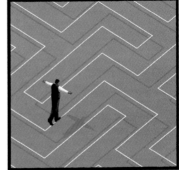

TOP: Famine in America, *National Labor Federation*   **ABOVE:** Teflon, *Fine Cooking Magazine*   **ABOVE:** Complexities of Risk Management

Gary Pierazzi

(530) 477-1950 garypierazzi.com

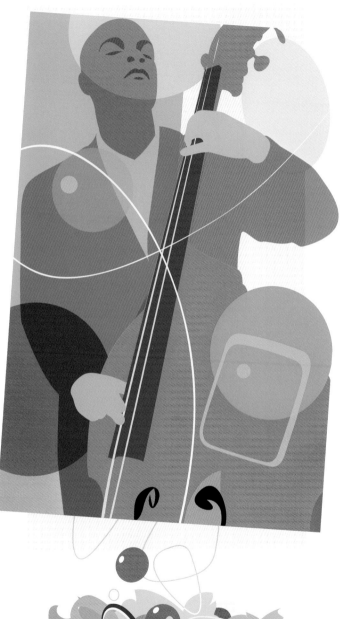

(530) 477-1950 GARYPIERAZZI.COM

TIM BARRALL

studio 212 243 9003   timbarrall.com   info@timbarrall.com   illiustration & digital enhancement

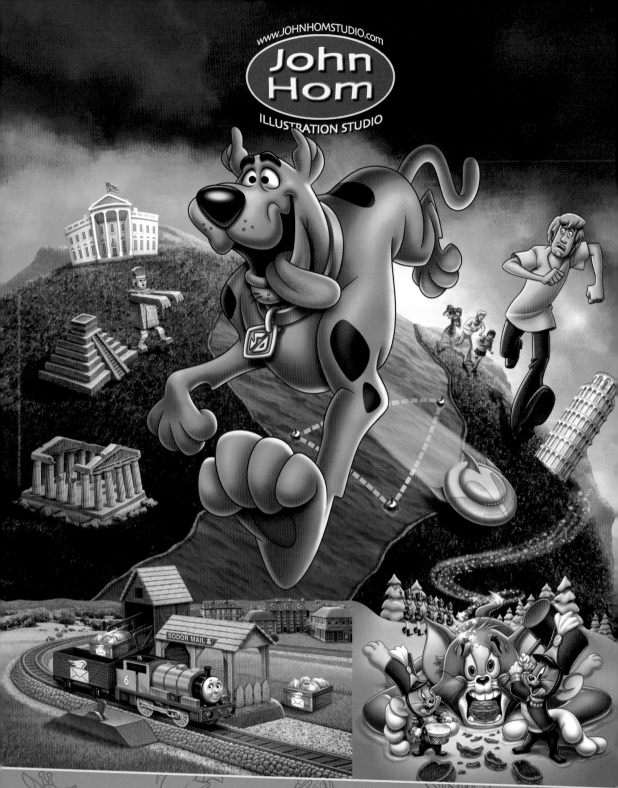

DAVE SEELEY

DO YOUR DUTY!

ENLIST TODAY!

PETER BOLLINGER

ERWIN MADRID

212 333 2551

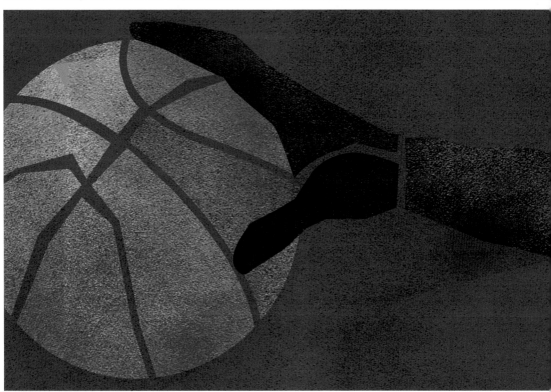

ROCCO MALATESTA

CLIFF NIELSEN

212 333 2551

JULIANA NEUFELD

IAN KELTIE

ALAN BROOKS

RAFAEL SARMENTO

SHANNON ASSOCIATES.COM

PER HAAGENSEN

BLAKE MORROW

JULIANA KOLESOVA

PASCAL CAMPION

212 333 2551

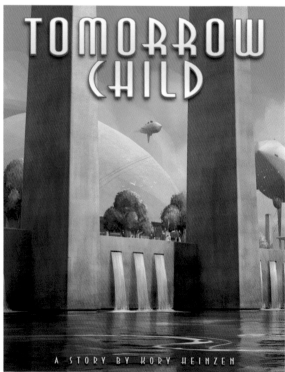

KORY HEINZEN

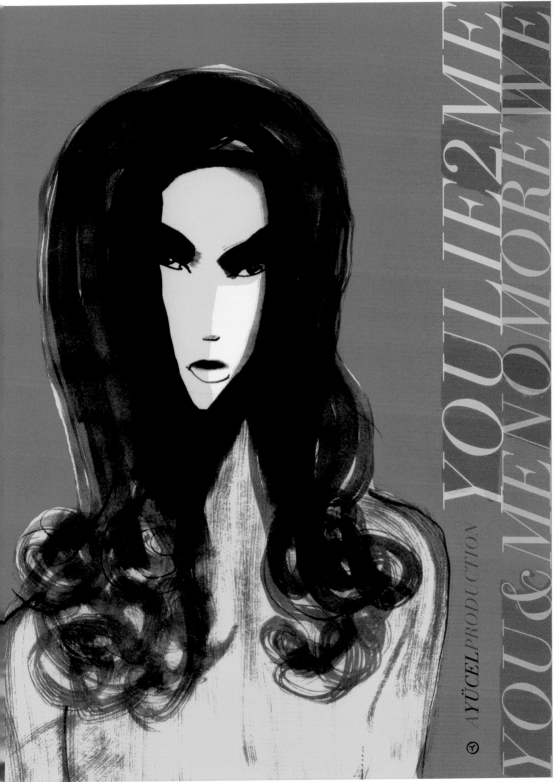

YOU LIE 2 ME
ME NO MORE WE
YOU & ME
YOU & ME NO MORE WE

Ⓨ A YÜCEL PRODUCTION

YUCEL

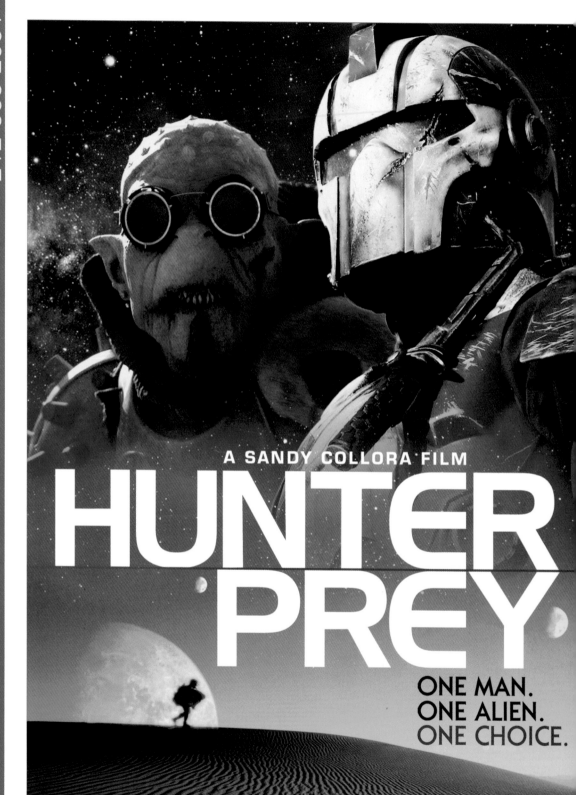

212 333 2551

A SANDY COLLORA FILM

HUNTER PREY

ONE MAN.
ONE ALIEN.
ONE CHOICE.

SPORK UNLIMITED

MICHAEL KOELSCH

212 333 2551

OWEN RICHARDSON

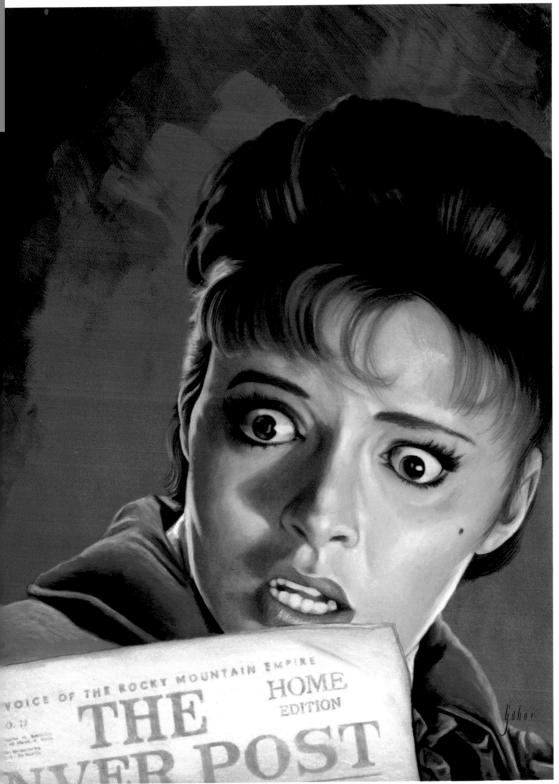

VOICE OF THE ROCKY MOUNTAIN EMPIRE

HOME
EDITION

THE
NVER POST

Gabor

TIM GABOR

DOUG HOLGATE

JOHN JOVEN

LISA HENDERLING

GLIN DIBLEY

JOHN JAY

CRYSSY CHEUNG

IKER AYESTERAN

JUICE FAST LOVE

kale beets carrots radishes
pink lady apples spinach
bok choy lemon cantaloupe
celery blueberries watermelon

MONIKA ROE

212 333 2551

20 anos do Centro Cultural Banco do Brasil. Faz diferença ser cliente de um banco que leva cultura para todo o país.

Pensar na cultura do brasileiro é pensar numa riqueza sem igual, onde milhares de formas, cores e ritmos se misturam em uma nação única. Nos Centros Culturais Banco do Brasil você encontra sempre uma programação assim: diversificada, criativa, onde cada brasileiro pode se sentir representado e, principalmente, estimulado.

Banco do Brasil. Faz diferença ter um banco todo seu.

bb.com.br/cultura

BANCO DA CULTURA

GUILHERME MARCONI

MURILO MACIEL

JON PROCTOR

212 333 2551

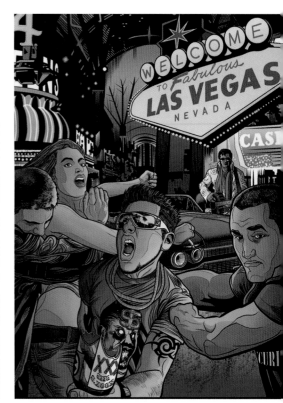

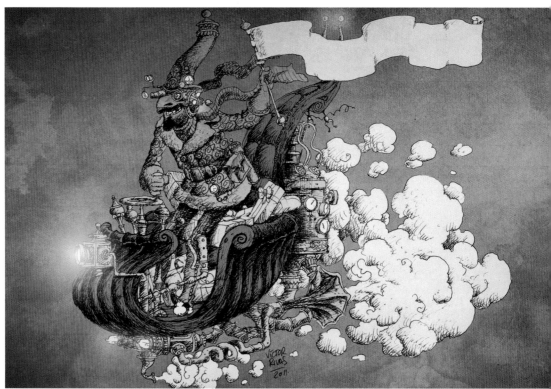

VICTOR RIVAS

CRAIG PHILLIPS

TRISTAN ELWELL

ROBERT HUNT

OMAR RAYYAN

JENNIFER L. MEYER

JIM MADSEN

ANTONIO JAVIER CAPARO

212 333 2551

STEPHEN GILPIN

Turkey Monster Thanksgiving

Anne Warren Smith

TUESDAY MOURNING

SHANE REBENSCHIED

DAVE PHILLIPS

212 333 2551

PATRICK FARICY

DAN ANDREASEN

JIMMY HOLDER

MORT DRUCKER

DAVID LEONARD

212 333 2551

ALEXANDERSEN

BARRETT

BATES

BELL

CALO

CASTALEO

CIMATORIBUS

CORTS

CURREY

CURTIS

FRANCIS

GUERLAIS

HAJDINJAK

HALE

HALEY

HALL

HANSEN

HENRY

HIBBERT

JACK

KIM

LAUGESEN

LEICK

LINTERN

MCGUIRE

MITCHELL

MONESCILLO

NGUYEN

O'KIF

OBERDIECK

OLSON

ONG

PARKS

ROOS

SAKAMOTO

SCALES

SHROADES

SIMON

SULLIVAN

WAKEFIELD

KID
shannon

Featuring over 150 premier children's book illustrators

OLYMPIC PENINSULA
WASHINGTON STATE — The DEPARTMENT of DEPENDABILITY
Powerful engines get the job done.

With a DD15, it's just a walk in the park.
CONTINENTAL DIVIDE
LOVELAND PASS, COLO — The DEPARTMENT of MASSIVE TORQUE

Out here, you need a truck that's built to take it.
STUART HIGHWAY
NORTHERN TERRITORY AUSTRALIA — The DEPARTMENT of NEVER QUITS
ROAD TRAIN

Power, durability and a never-say-die attitude.
HOOVER DAM BYPASS
ARIZONA · NEVADA — The DEPARTMENT of BRUTE FORCE

Moving a highway underground takes a real work truck.
THE BIG DIG
BOSTON, MASSACHUSETTS — The DEPARTMENT of WICKED TOUGH

240,000 metric tonnes of gold, silver and copper mined each day.
GRASBERG MINE
PUNCAK JAYA, INDONESIA — The DEPARTMENT of MOVING MOUNTAINS

Incredible performance, no matter what the conditions.
SEA-TO-SKY HIGHWAY
WHISTLER, BC — The DEPARTMENT of GETTING IT DONE

A billion barrels just waiting there.
ALBERTA TAR SANDS
ALBERTA, CANADA — The DEPARTMENT of NO CRYBABIES

BOB KAYGANICH

MARK COLLINS

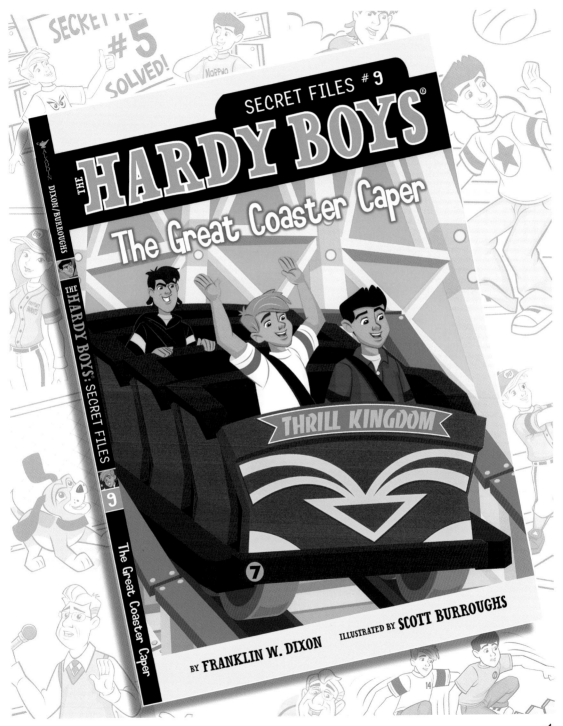

SECRET FILES # 9

THE HARDY BOYS®

The Great Coaster Caper

THRILL KINGDOM

BY FRANKLIN W. DIXON   ILLUSTRATED BY SCOTT BURROUGHS

215.232.6666   www.illustrationOnLine.com   DEBORAH WOLFE LTD

RALPH VOLTZ

DAN MCGEEHAN

215.232.6666   www.illustrationOnLine.com   DEBORAH WOLFE LTD

AMY CARTWRIGHT

NANCY HARRISON

WATERMARK

GREG COPELAND

ROSS JONES

AMY WUMMER

RICHARD CARBAJAL

TED HAMMOND

CINDY REVELL

215.232.6666   www.illustrationOnLine.com   DEBORAH WOLFE LTD

233

Anzalone & Avarella Studios LLC
973 300 9354 lori@lorianzalone.com lorianzalone.com avarella.com

howard mcwilliam

BLASCO CREATIVE ARTISTS

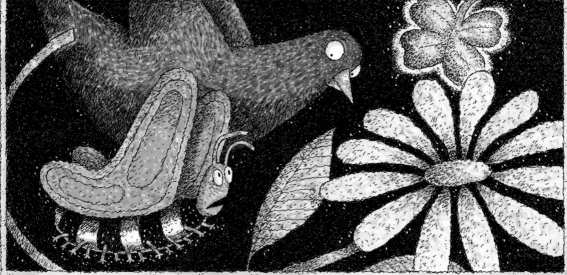

Book Interiors
Created for
**There Was An Old Lady
Who Swallowed A Clover**
By Lucille Colandro
Scholastic Publisher

JARED LEE

www.jaredlee.com

Jared Lee started his
free-lance career in 1970
working with national
ad agencies, magazines,
and book publishers.
He has created over 100
children's books with
29,000,000 in print.

TEL: (513) 932-2154   jaredlee@go-concepts.com   FAX: (513) 932-9389

KEVIN
SPROULS

Wall Street Portraits

KEVIN@SPROULS.COM   PH. 609.965.4795
WWW.SPROULS.COM

Smart party girls take *taxis* and use protection.

smart.
karen greenberg
illustration
646.894.5796
karengreenberg.com

Mark Smith

SALZMAN
international

415.285.8267   salzint.com   212.997.0115

Debbie Tilley

Denise Hilton Campbell

Niklas Asker

Kent Barton

James Bennett

Tim Bower

Scott Brundage

Maria Corte Maidagan

Doug Cowan

Paul Cox

Kinuko Y. Craft

Eric Drooker

Michał Dziekan

Thomas Ehrestmann

Jon Foster

Chris Gall

Rudy Gutierrez

John Hersey

Tyler Jacobson

David Johnson

Gary Kelley

Murray Kimber

dward Kinsella III

Dongyun Lee

Gregory Manchess

Ricardo Martínez

ohn Mattos

Goñi Montes

Yan Nascimbene

Tran Nguyen

F Payne

Bill Sanderson

Jason Seiler

Douglas Smith

ark T. Smith

Guy Stauber

Chase Stone

Mark Summers

hris Whetzel

Andrew R. Wright

Ted Wright

RICHARD SOLOMON™
ARTISTS REPRESENTATIVE, LLC

212 223 9545 · 917 841 1333
richard@richardsolomon.com
www.richardsolomon.com

110 E 30th Street
Suite 501
New York, NY 10016

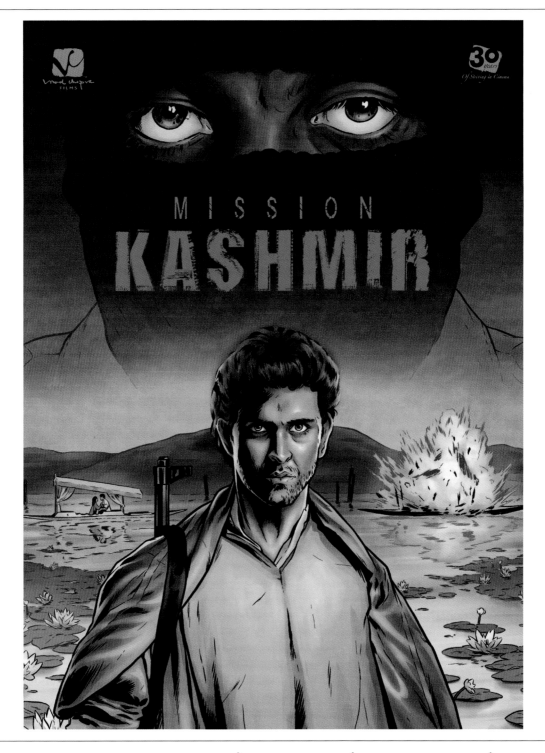

**NIKLAS
ASKER**

JAMES
BENNETT

RICHARD SOLOMON™
ARTISTS REPRESENTATIVE

212 223 9545 · 917 841 1333
www.richardsolomon.com
richard@richardsolomon.com

110 E 30th St,
Ste. 501
New York, NY 1001

PAUL
COX

 RICHARD
SOLOMON™
ARTISTS REPRESENTATIVE

212 223 9545 · 917 841 1333
www.richardsolomon.com
richard@richardsolomon.com

110 E 30th St,
Ste. 501
New York, NY 1001

ERIC
BROOKER

RICHARD
SOLOMON™
ARTISTS REPRESENTATIVE

212 223 9545 · 917 841 1333
www.richardsolomon.com
richard@richardsolomon.com

110 E 30th St,
Ste. 501
New York, NY 10016

THOMAS
EHRETSMANN

 RICHARD
SOLOMON™
ARTISTS REPRESENTATIVE

212 223 9545 · 917 841 1333
www.richardsolomon.com
richard@richardsolomon.com

110 E 30th St,
Ste. 501
New York, NY 1001

CHRIS
GALL

 RICHARD SOLOMON™
ARTISTS REPRESENTATIVE

212 223 9545 · 917 841 1333
www.richardsolomon.com
richard@richardsolomon.com

110 E 30th St,
Ste. 501
New York, NY 1001

JUDY
GUTIERREZ

RICHARD
SOLOMON™
ARTISTS REPRESENTATIVE

212 223 9545 · 917 841 1333
www.richardsolomon.com
richard@richardsolomon.com

110 E 30th St,
Ste. 501
New York, NY 10016

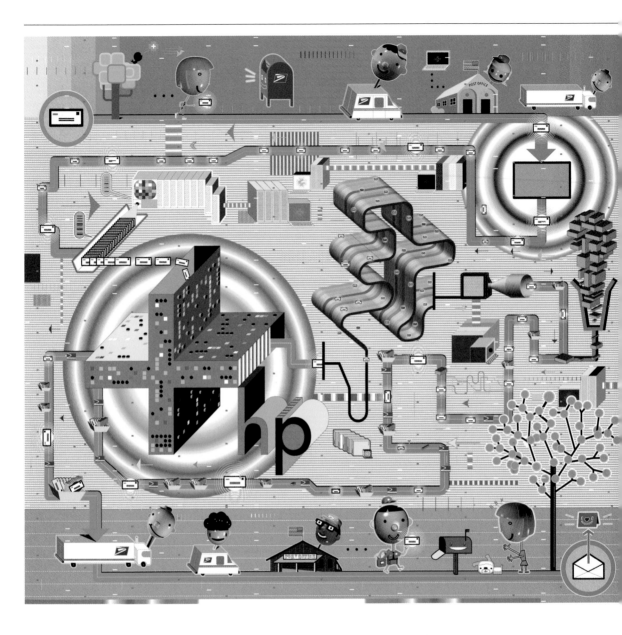

JOHN
HERSEY

3S RICHARD
SOLOMON™
ARTISTS REPRESENTATIVE

212 223 9545 · 917 841 1333
www.richardsolomon.com
richard@richardsolomon.com

110 E 30th St,
Ste. 501
New York, NY 100

TYLER
JACOBSON

RICHARD
SOLOMON™
ARTISTS REPRESENTATIVE

212 223 9545 · 917 841 1333
www.richardsolomon.com
richard@richardsolomon.com

110 E 30th St,
Ste. 501
New York, NY 10016

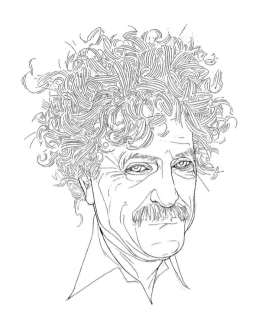

DAVID
JOHNSON

 RICHARD
SOLOMON™
ARTISTS REPRESENTATIVE

212 223 9545 · 917 841 1333
www.richardsolomon.com
richard@richardsolomon.com

110 E 30th St,
Ste. 501
New York, NY 100

ARY
ELLEY

 **RICHARD SOLOMON™** ARTISTS REPRESENTATIVE

212 223 9545 · 917 841 1333
www.richardsolomon.com
richard@richardsolomon.com

110 E 30th St,
Ste. 501
New York, NY 10016

DWARD
INSELLA III

RICHARD SOLOMON™
ARTISTS REPRESENTATIVE

212 223 9545 · 917 841 1333
www.richardsolomon.com
richard@richardsolomon.com

110 E 30th St,
Ste. 501
New York, NY 10016

**DONGYUN
LEE**

RICHARD SOLOMON™
ARTISTS REPRESENTATIVE

212 223 9545 · 917 841 1333
www.richardsolomon.com
richard@richardsolomon.com

110 E 30th St,
Ste. 501
New York, NY 100

GREGORY
MANCHESS

 RICHARD
SOLOMON™
ARTISTS REPRESENTATIVE

212 223 9545 · 917 841 1333
www.richardsolomon.com
richard@richardsolomon.com

110 E 30th St,
Ste. 501
New York, NY 10016

GOLDEN GATE BRIDGE
ART DECO SOCIETY OF CALIFORNIA

**JOHN
MATTOS**

RICHARD SOLOMON™
ARTISTS REPRESENTATIVE

212 223 9545 · 917 841 1333
www.richardsolomon.com
richard@richardsolomon.com

110 E 30th St,
Ste. 501
New York, NY 100

YAN
NASCIMBENE

 RICHARD
SOLOMON™
ARTISTS REPRESENTATIVE

212 223 9545 · 917 841 1333
www.richardsolomon.com
richard@richardsolomon.com

110 E 30th St,
Ste. 501
New York, NY 1001

C.F.
PAYNE

 RICHARD
SOLOMON™
ARTISTS REPRESENTATIVE

212 223 9545 · 917 841 1333
www.richardsolomon.com
richard@richardsolomon.com

110 E 30th St,
Ste. 501
New York, NY 10016

ASON
SEILER

 RICHARD
SOLOMON™
ARTISTS REPRESENTATIVE

212 223 9545 · 917 841 1333
www.richardsolomon.com
richard@richardsolomon.com

110 E 30th St,
Ste. 501
New York, NY 10016

**DOUGLAS
SMITH**

 **RICHARD
SOLOMON**™
ARTISTS REPRESENTATIVE

212 223 9545 · 917 841 1333
www.richardsolomon.com
richard@richardsolomon.com

110 E 30th St,
Ste. 501
New York, NY 1001

ABSOLUT SMITH.

MARK T.
MITH

CHASE
STONE

RICHARD
SOLOMON™
ARTISTS REPRESENTATIVE

212 223 9545 · 917 841 1333
www.richardsolomon.com
richard@richardsolomon.com

110 E 30th St,
Ste. 501
New York, NY 1001

MARK
SUMMERS

 RICHARD
SOLOMON™
ARTISTS REPRESENTATIVE

212 223 9545 · 917 841 1333
www.richardsolomon.com
richard@richardsolomon.com

110 E 30th St,
Ste. 501
New York, NY 10016

CHRIS
WHETZEL

RICHARD SOLOMON™
ARTISTS REPRESENTATIVE

212 223 9545 · 917 841 1333
www.richardsolomon.com
richard@richardsolomon.com

110 E 30th St,
Ste. 501
New York, NY 100

THE
SADDLERY
COWBOY BAR
&
STEAKHOUSE
TORREY, UTAH

ED
WRIGHT

 RICHARD
SOLOMON™
ARTISTS REPRESENTATIVE

212 223 9545 · 917 841 1333
www.richardsolomon.com
richard@richardsolomon.com

110 E 30th St,
Ste. 501
New York, NY 10016

randy@randylyhus.com

Russ Charpentier
Classical Maps & Illustration

The Scale of Miles

707.552.7094
russrc@earthlink.net

CHARPENTIER GRAPHICS
workbook.com/portfolios/charpentier

charpentiergraphics.com
theispot.com/artist/charpentier

scott pollack   516-921-1908   **scottpollack.com**

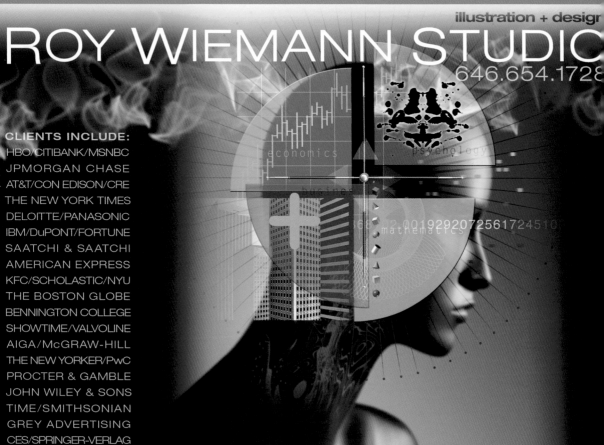

DOUG BOWLES illustration

913-385-0462 dbowles@earthlink.net

www.dougbowles.net

LINDGREN ◼ SMITH
{212} 397-7330

Jim Salvati

LINDGRENSMITH.COM
INFO@LSILLUSTRATION.COM

LINDGREN ≈ SMITH   *Michael Paraskevas*   LINDGRENSMITH.COM
{212} 397-7330   INFO@LSILLUSTRATION.COM

LINDGREN ◆ SMITH
{212} 397-7330

Miles Hyman

LINDGRENSMITH.COM
INFO@LSILLUSTRATION.COM

LINDGREN ▬ SMITH
{212} 397-7330

Jamey Christoph

LINDGRENSMITH.COM
INFO@LSILLUSTRATION.COM

LINDGREN ▬ SMITH
{212} 397-7330

Kim Johnson

LINDGRENSMITH.COM
INFO@LSILLUSTRATION.COM

291

THE SATURDAY EVENING POST

Founded A.D. 1728 by Benjamin Franklin

AMERICA GOES DANCE CRAZY!
Page 40

BONUS!
LUSCIOUS
HOLIDAY RECIPES!

THE QUIETEST
PLACE ON EARTH

ROCKWELL'S
CHRISTMAS
VISION

Pyle

LINDGREN ◼ SMITH
{212} 397-7330

Susan Leopold

LINDGRENSMITH.COM
INFO@LSILLUSTRATION.COM

LINDGREN ⬛ SMITH
{212} 397-7330

Jeff Bennett

LINDGRENSMITH.COM
INFO@LSILLUSTRATION.COM

LINDGREN ◥ SMITH
{212} 397-7330

Jerome Studer

LINDGRENSMITH.COM
INFO@LSILLUSTRATION.COM

LINDGREN ◼ SMITH *Christiane Beauregard* LINDGRENSMITH.COM
{212} 397-7330 INFO@LSILLUSTRATION.COM

annibetts
annibetts.com

Courtesy Garmin, L[...]

helenravenhillrepresents
tel 816.333.0744 web ravenhill.net

David Moore RETROREPS.COM T. 310 670-5300

STEVE VANCE REPRESENTED BY MARTHAPRODUCTIONS.COM
MARTHA@MARTHAPRODUCTIONS.COM • 310-670-5300

PATRICK STEFANSKI
3D Design & Illustration

hello@patrickstefanski.com
(201)855-6022

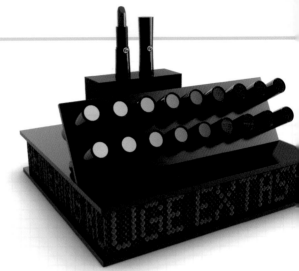

mari araki illustration & lettering
REPRESENTED BY
Jim Hanson Artist Agent LTD / jimhanson.com

mark stutzman

Eloqui.COM

At eloqui.com see
how artwork can bring
personal style
to your brand.

THE ILLUMINATE BULB
Stockholm, Sweden
merchandise | advertising
Original art 20" x 30"
watercolor, gouache & airbrush

Eloqui is a studio devoted to illustration

100 G STREET | MTN. LAKE PARK MD 21550 | 301 334 4086
eloqui.com ⟁ markstutzman.com ✉ mark@eloqui.com

308

NO WIN
NO FLEA

gs GARY SWIFT STUDIOS

+44 (0) 1977 646431 | gary@garyswift.com
www.garyswift.com

Lucky

Come and **say hello!**

LANCE
JACKSON

lancejackson.net
noirture.com
ljackson09.blogspot.com
925.253.3131
lancejackson09@gmail.com

CARLA BAUER WOODCUTS CARLABAUER@EARTHLINK.NET 212 807 830

Der Spiegel

nputerWorld

Angie's List

nSponsor

Angie's List

Marian He

Marian He

Arcobaleno

Pondiche

Landor

InAdv

pyrus

Papyrus

Andrews and Blaine

Petal Pushers

Coming Up Roses

Catherine R. Daly   SCHOLASTIC   Scholastic

emiliano ponzi

magnet reps | artist representatives [866] 390-5656 art@magnetreps.

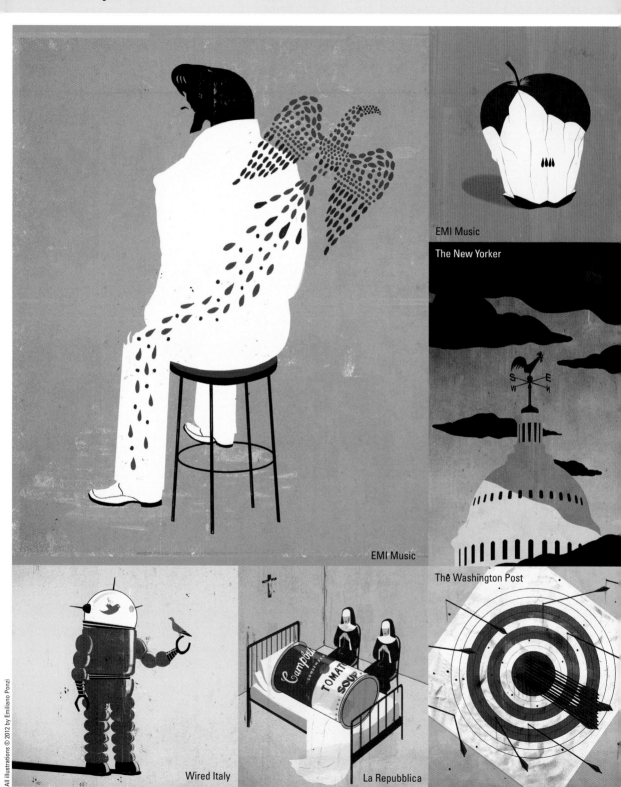

EMI Music

The New Yorker

EMI Music

The Washington Post

Wired Italy

La Repubblica

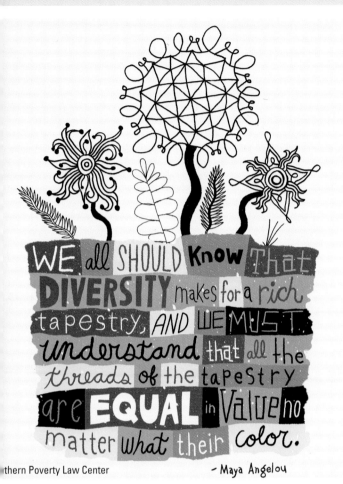

WE all SHOULD Know That DIVERSITY makes for a rich tapestry, AND WE MUST understand that all the threads of the tapestry are EQUAL in Value no matter what their color.

— Maya Angelou

thern Poverty Law Center

ELKANO BROWNING CREAM Bohemia

Draft FCB

Keep the FUN Growing BINGO

SWING into SPRING
SPECIALS of the MONTH

Light Done Right Edgy veggie Dishes

30 MINUTE MEALS
• Caesar Pesto Pasta
• Pea & Carrot Soup
• Risotto Primavera

You're INVITED!
Sunday Brunch with Alex Guarnaschelli

Every Day with Rachael Ray

♥ HandLettering

TMG Media

HOW Magazine

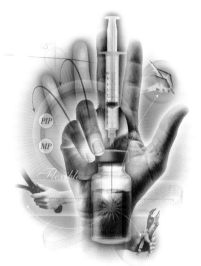

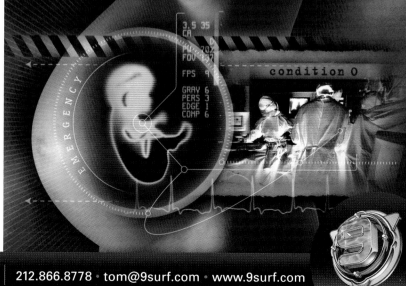

EXTERIOR RENDERING

VEHICLE CREATION

ACTION FIGURES

PRODUCT PRESENTATIONS

SERGEY GREY
WWW.INTERACTIVEIDEA.NET

TECHNICAL ILLUSTRATIONS

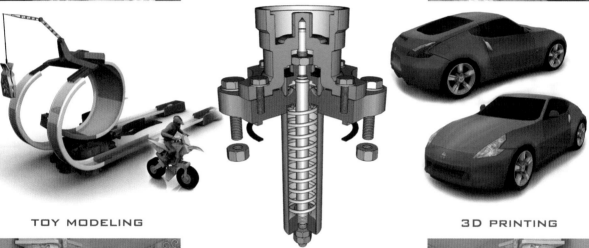

TOY MODELING

3D PRINTING

INTERIOR RENDERING

904-962-3274
PROJECT@INTERACTIVEIDEA.NET

tracy lee stum | 3-d chalk art
3-d | advertising | marketing | events | commissions

tracy lee stum | 3-d chalk art

3-d | advertising | marketing | events | commissions

contact Justin Sudds   604.734.5945   tracyleestum.com

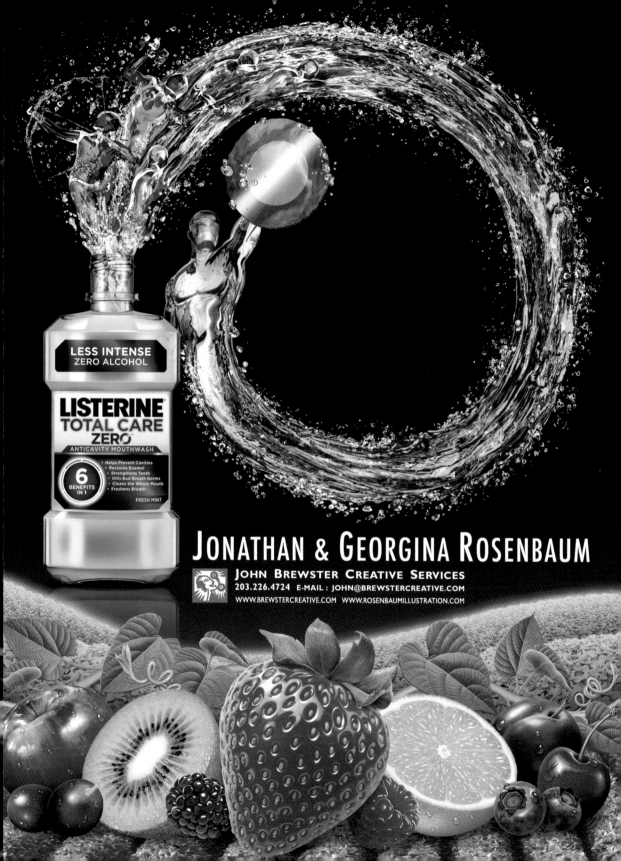

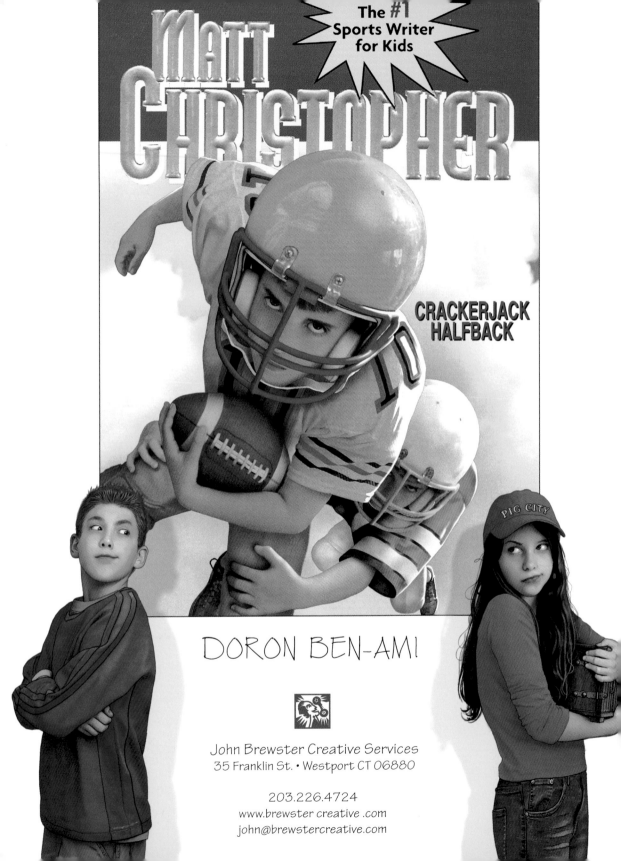

JAMES SILVANI

(808)874-8759
www.silvaniart.com
james@silvaniart.com

John Brewster Creative Services
(203)226-4724
www.brewstercreative.com
john@brewstercreative.com

SHARIF TARABAY

JOHN BREWSTER CREATIVE SERVICES

PHONE: 203.226.4724   WEB: BREWSTERCREATIVE.COM

E-MAIL: JOHN@BREWSTERCREATIVE.COM

ILLUSTRATORS
PARTNERSHIP
OF AMERICA

LANE DU PONT

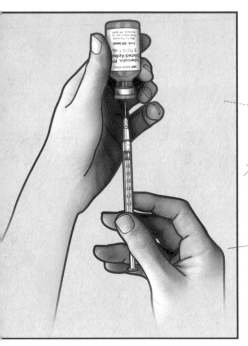

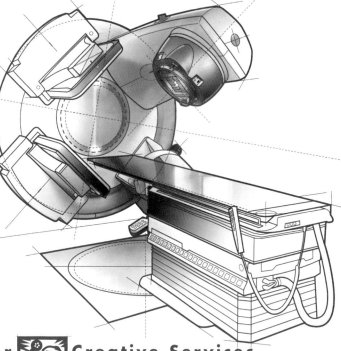

John Brewster Creative Services

Phone 203.226.4724 Fax 203.454.9904
John@brewstercreative.com www.brewstercreative.com

416-699-1525 **DAN F🔻LL** dfell@sympatico.ca

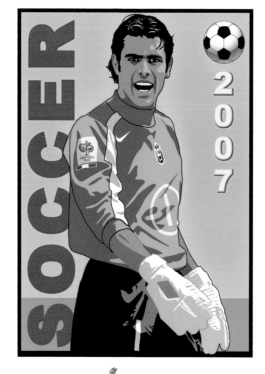

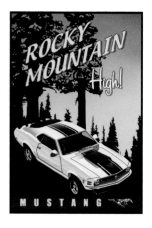

www.danfell.com

Maurice Vellekoop

Alëna Skarina

16.703.1913   51 Camden Street, Main Floor, Toronto, Ontario M5V 1V2   visit us online: www.reactor.ca

R.O. Blechman

Tracey Wood

MARY ANN SMITH

www.maryannsmithwork.com | 212.691.3570 | maryann.smith14@verizon.net

BARBARA SPURLL 1·800·989·3123 WWW.BARBARASPURLL.COM

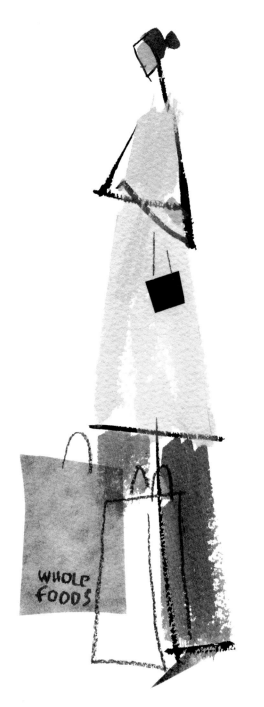

Nishan
Nishan Akgulian illustration
www.nishanakgulian.com

Comm. by Scientific American Magazine.

Self-initiated.

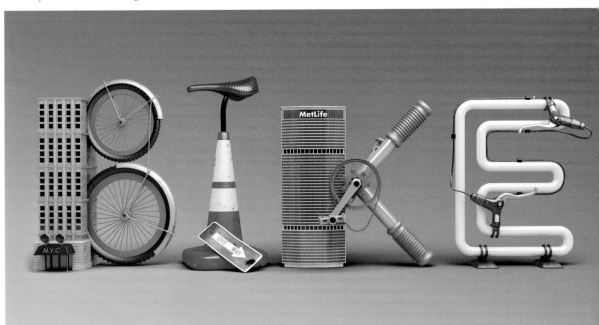

Comm. by Fry & Torres at DeBrain.

Chris Labrooy

début **art** • Illustrators, Photographers and Fine Artists Agents. 30 Tottenham Street, London, W1T 4RJ. United Kingdom
Tel: 01144 20 7636 1064. Fax: 01144 20 7580 7017. **The Coningsby Gallery** • Tel: 01144 20 7636 7478

email: **info@debutart.com** • **www.debutart.com**

début ar

début **art** • Illustrators, Photographers and Fine Artists Agents

30 Tottenham Street, London, W1T 4RJ. United Kingdom

Tel: 01144 20 7636 1064. Fax: 01144 20 7580 7017

The Coningsby Gallery • Tel: 01144 20 7636 7478

email: **info@debutart.com** • **www.debutart.com**

the coningsby gallery

Since 1985, *début* **art** (based in London, England and now with offices in New York and Paris) has proactively sought out leading contemporary image-makers & clients who create original, progressive and commercially successful media material. Today, *début* **art** and the highly artistic illustrators it promotes, are widely regarded, both in the UK and around the world, as representing one of the finest and most contemporary talent groupings in the field of illustration.

début **art** and the illustrators it markets have successfully undertaken assignments worldwide for very many companies that are leaders in their fields including: Microsoft, Apple, Coca-Cola, Proctor and Gamble, Samsung, Levi's, Nokia, Rolls-Royce, BP, Shell, Nike, The Chicago Mercantile Exchange, The NYSE, The London Stock Exchange, Bloomberg, American Express, Barclaycard, HSBC, IBM, British Airways, Unilever, Harrods, Selfridges, Macy's (New York), Topshop, Verizon, Lucas Inc, The Royal Opera House (London), Universal Music, Sony, Miller, Burton, Harper Collins, The Wall Street Journal, The New York Times, The Times (London), Le Monde, The Economist, The Financial Times, Vogue, Cosmopolitan and National Geographic Magazine.

Full portfolios for every artist can be reviewed and requested via our web site at **www.debutart.com**

The Coningsby Gallery stages some 30 exhibitions per year by selected leading illustrators, photographers and fine artists. Review of previous exhibitions, a look at upcoming shows and a photo tour of the gallery itself can be accessed at **www.coningsbygallery.com**

Contact: Andrew Coningsby, Samuel Summerskill, Jonathan Hedley and Rhiannon Lloyd

Alan Aldridge	Paul Davis	Ilovedust	Sophie Marsham	Nick Reddyhoff	Triggerfish 21
Arno	Carol del Angel	Infomen	Kim McGillivray	The Red Dress	Alex Trochut
Andrew Baker	Pierre Doucin	Jacey	Vince McIndoe	Redseal	Jim Tsinganos
Istvan Banyai	Barry Downard	Jackdaw	Wesley Merritt	Cath Riley	Vault49
Gary Bates	Katie Edwards	Sarah Jones	Justin Metz	Craig Robinson	Stephanie von Reiswitz
Jon Berkeley	El Señor	Alan Kitching	Gabriel Moreno	Kerry Roper	Jeff Wack
Chris Bianchi	Tim Ellis	Eley Kishimoto	Patrick Morgan	Saeko	Stephan Walter
Jacquie Boyd	Sam Falconer	Viktor Koen	Morten Morland	Serge Seidlitz	Neil Webb
Norm Breyfogle	Jo Fernihough	Ronald Kurniawan	Huntley/Muir	Seripop	Jane Webster
Jon Burgerman	Flatliner	Christina K	Chris Nurse	Shape & Colour	Joe Wilson
Oliver Burston	Peter Grundy	Yuko Kondo	Kevin O'Keefe	Craig Shuttlewood	Oscar Wilson
Benedict Campbell	Sarah Hanson	Kolchoz	Martin O'Neill	Niels Shoe Meulman	Alex Williamson
Danny Capozzi	Jethro Haynes	La Boca	Alex Pang	Michel Streich	Tina Zellmer
James Carey	Sarah Haywood	Chris Labrooy	Paper Work	Sroop Sunar	Jurgen Ziewe
Celyn	Matt Herring	Yann Legendre	Mac Premo	Tado	Vasili Zorin
Russell Cobb	Oliver Hibert	Neil Leslie	Pietari Posti	James Taylor	
Matthew Cooper	Nanette Hoogslag	Lie-ins & Tigers	Chris Price	The Studio	
Peter Crowther	Sarah Howell	Andy Lovell	Paul Price	Yehrin Tong	
Marta Cerda	Frazer Hudson	Harry Malt	Peter Quinnell	Sophie Toulouse	
Matthew Dartford	Drawn Ideas	Stephane Manel	Steve Rawlings	Dominic Trevett	

'Beauty is truth, truth beauty'
John Keats

Comm. for Infiniti.

Comm. by Z-Life Magazine.

Comm. for Taco Bell.

Jackdaw

début **art** • Illustrators, Photographers and Fine Artists Agents. 30 Tottenham Street, London, W1T 4RJ. United Kingdom
Tel: 01144 20 7636 1064. Fax: 01144 20 7580 7017. **The Coningsby Gallery** • Tel: 01144 20 7636 7478

email: **info@debutart.com** • **www.debutart.com**

Comm. by Nike.

Comm. by L.A. Magazine.

Comm. for Fiat.

Gabriel Moreno

début **art** • Illustrators, Photographers and Fine Artists Agents. 30 Tottenham Street, London, W1T 4RJ. United Kingdom
Tel: 01144 20 7636 1064. Fax: 01144 20 7580 7017. **The Coningsby Gallery** • Tel: 01144 20 7636 7478

Email: **info@debutart.com** • **www.debutart.com**

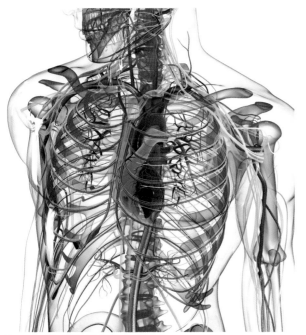

Comm. by Men's Health Magazine.

Comm. by Men's Fitness Magazine.

Comm. by Martha Stuart Living Magazine.

Comm. by F1 Magazine.

Peter Crowther Associates

début **art** • Illustrators, Photographers and Fine Artists Agents. 30 Tottenham Street, London, W1T 4RJ. United Kingdom
Tel: 01144 20 7636 1064. Fax: 01144 20 7580 7017. **The Coningsby Gallery** • Tel: 01144 20 7636 7478

email: **info@debutart.com** • **www.debutart.com**

Comm. by Fortune Magazine.

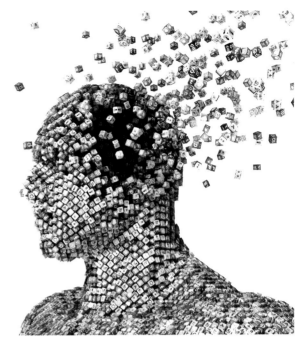

Comm. by Men's Fitness Magazine.

Comm. by Real Deals Magazine.

Comm. by Bicycling Magazine.

Comm. for ABSA Bank.

Comm. for Pringles.

Self-initiated.

Barry Downard

début **art** • Illustrators, Photographers and Fine Artists Agents. 30 Tottenham Street, London, W1T 4RJ. United Kingdom
Tel: 01144 20 7636 1064. Fax: 01144 20 7580 7017. **The Coningsby Gallery** • Tel: 01144 20 7636 7478

email: **info@debutart.com** • **www.debutart.com**

début **art**

Comm. for Phones4U.

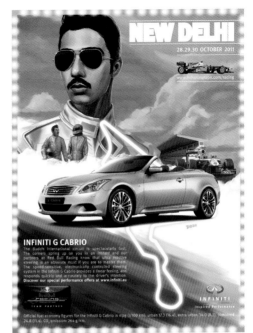

Comm. for Infiniti.

Comm. for 'The Bear' Stage Play.

Comm. by Esquire Magazine.

The Red Dress

ébut **art** • Illustrators, Photographers and Fine Artists Agents. 30 Tottenham Street, London, W1T 4RJ. United Kingdom
el: 01144 20 7636 1064. Fax: 01144 20 7580 7017. **The Coningsby Gallery** • Tel: 01144 20 7636 7478

mail: **info@debutart.com** • **www.debutart.com**

Comm. for SHOP Magazine (Italy).

Comm. by Scientific American Magazine.

Comm. for IB World Magazine.

Comm. for Brunswick Review.

Neil Webb

début **art** • Illustrators, Photographers and Fine Artists Agents. 30 Tottenham Street, London, W1T 4RJ. United Kingdom
Tel: 01144 20 7636 1064. Fax: 01144 20 7580 7017. **The Coningsby Gallery** • Tel: 01144 20 7636 7478

email: **info@debutart.com** • **www.debutart.com**

début **art**

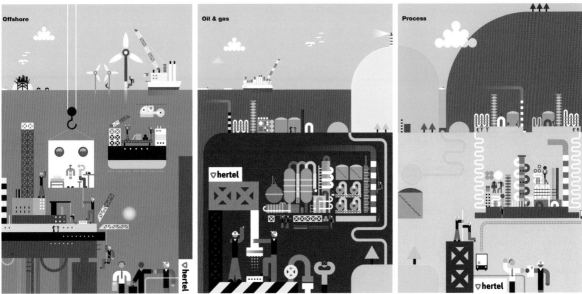

Comm. for Hertel.

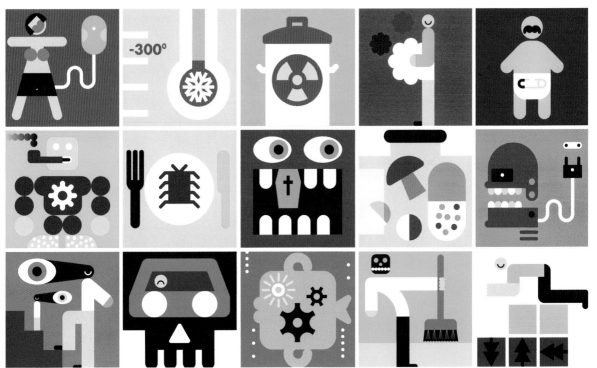

Comm. by Reader's Digest.

Peter Grundy

début **art** • Illustrators, Photographers and Fine Artists Agents. 30 Tottenham Street, London, W1T 4RJ. United Kingdom
Tel: 01144 20 7636 1064. Fax: 01144 20 7580 7017. **The Coningsby Gallery** • Tel: 01144 20 7636 7478

Email: **info@debutart.com** • **www.debutart.com**

début **art**

Comm. for Mountain Dew.

Comm. by ESPN Magazine.

Comm. by Volvo Magazine.

Comm. by APEX Magazine.

James Carey

début **art** • Illustrators, Photographers and Fine Artists Agents. 30 Tottenham Street, London, W1T 4RJ. United Kingdom
Tel: 01144 20 7636 1064. Fax: 01144 20 7580 7017. **The Coningsby Gallery** • Tel: 01144 20 7636 7478

email: **info@debutart.com** • **www.debutart.com**

début **art**

Comm. by Duke University Magazine.

Comm. by New Scientist Magazine.

Comm. for BP.

Comm. by Military Officer's Association of America Magazine.

Alex Williamson

début **art** • Illustrators, Photographers and Fine Artists Agents. 30 Tottenham Street, London, W1T 4RJ. United Kingdom
Tel: 01144 20 7636 1064. Fax: 01144 20 7580 7017. **The Coningsby Gallery** • Tel: 01144 20 7636 7478

mail: **info@debutart.com** • **www.debutart.com**

Self-initiated.

Comm. by Atlanta Magazine.

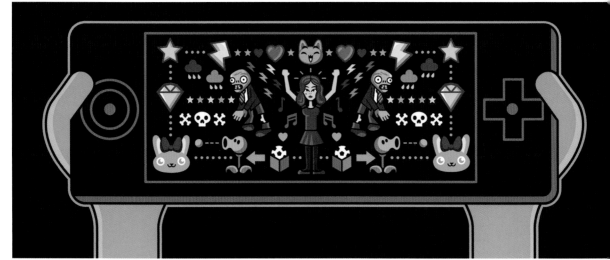

Comm. by Fortune Magazine.

Serge Seidlitz

début **art** • Illustrators, Photographers and Fine Artists Agents. 30 Tottenham Street, London, W1T 4RJ. United Kingdom
Tel: 01144 20 7636 1064. Fax: 01144 20 7580 7017. **The Coningsby Gallery** • Tel: 01144 20 7636 7478

email: **info@debutart.com** • **www.debutart.com**

mm. by Educational Insights.

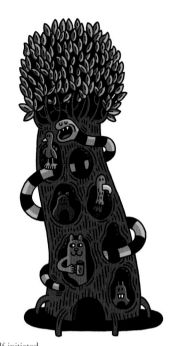

Self-initiated.

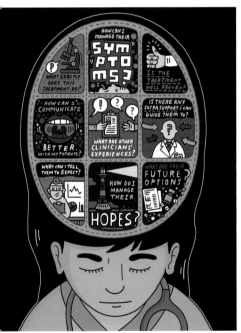

mm. for Rover.

Comm. for Red Lobster Restaurants.

début **art**

Comm. by Computer Arts Magazine.

Vault49

début **art** • Illustrators, Photographers and Fine Artists Agents. 30 Tottenham Street, London, W1T 4RJ. United Kingdom
Tel: 01144 20 7636 1064. Fax: 01144 20 7580 7017. **The Coningsby Gallery** • Tel: 01144 20 7636 7478

email: **info@debutart.com** • **www.debutart.com**

SARULA

Sarula {să'rōō-lä}
Black Widow Honey

Comm. by Express.

FALL GETAWAYS

Comm. by Boston Magazine.

LEADING PLAYER · DAY · VOTE
DARRON THOMAS · 002 · 50K

HEISMAN

LANDRY JONES · DENARD ROBINSON · KELLEN MORRE JR · MARCUS LATTIMORE · LAMICHAEL JAMES · DARRON THOMAS · JACQUIZZ RODGERS · BRANDON WEEDEN · TREY BURTON · TAYLOR MARTINEZ

10/2 · SLIDE

Comm. for Nissan.

Comm. by Computer Arts Magazine.

début **art**

Comm. by Popular Science Magazine.

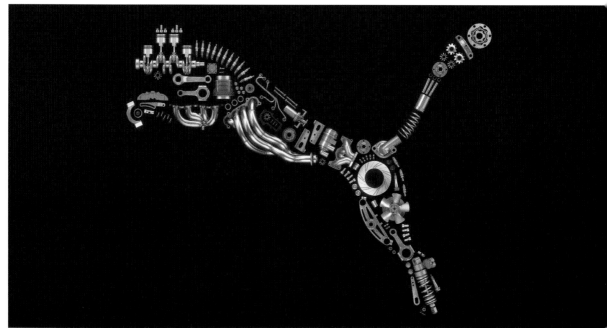

Comm. for Puma.

Matt Dartford / Flip CG

début **art** • Illustrators, Photographers and Fine Artists Agents. 30 Tottenham Street, London, W1T 4RJ. United Kingdom
Tel: 01144 20 7636 1064. Fax: 01144 20 7580 7017. **The Coningsby Gallery** • Tel: 01144 20 7636 7478

email: **info@debutart.com** • **www.debutart.com**

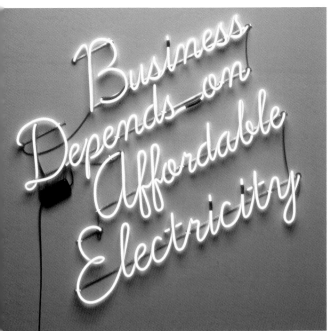

omm. for Tristate.

Comm. for Stella Artois.

omm. by Guitar World Magazine.

Self-initiated.

début art

357

Comm. by Disney.

Comm. by Moneyweek Magazine.

Comm. for Ted Baker Eyewear.

Comm. for Undiz France.

Arno

début **art** • Illustrators, Photographers and Fine Artists Agents. 30 Tottenham Street, London, W1T 4RJ. United Kingdom
Tel: 01144 20 7636 1064. Fax: 01144 20 7580 7017. **The Coningsby Gallery** • Tel: 01144 20 7636 7478

email: **info@debutart.com** • **www.debutart.com**

début ar

omm. by Fortune Magazine.

Comm. by The South Bank Centre (London).

omm. by Toronto Life Magazine.

Comm. by Vanity Fair Magazine.

imes Taylor

but **art** • Illustrators, Photographers and Fine Artists Agents. 30 Tottenham Street, London, W1T 4RJ. United Kingdom
el: 01144 20 7636 1064. Fax: 01144 20 7580 7017. **The Coningsby Gallery** • Tel: 01144 20 7636 7478

nail: **info@debutart.com** • **www.debutart.com**

début **art**

CARNIVAL
OF THE
COCKTAIL

Comm. for 42Below Vodka.

Self-initiated.

Comm. for Maharishi.

Comm. for Bombay Sapphire Gin.

Yehrin Tong

début **art** • Illustrators, Photographers and Fine Artists Agents. 30 Tottenham Street, London, W1T 4RJ. United Kingdom
Tel: 01144 20 7636 1064.   Fax: 01144 20 7580 7017. **The Coningsby Gallery** • Tel: 01144 20 7636 7478

email: **info@debutart.com** • **www.debutart.com**

début ar

Comm. by Alexander McQueen.

Self-initiated.

Comm. by Dash Magazine.

Self-initiated.

Patrick Morgan

début **art** • Illustrators, Photographers and Fine Artists Agents. 30 Tottenham Street, London, W1T 4RJ. United Kingdom
Tel: 01144 20 7636 1064. Fax: 01144 20 7580 7017. **The Coningsby Gallery** • Tel: 01144 20 7636 7478

Email: **info@debutart.com** • **www.debutart.com**

Comm. by Scholastic Publishing.

Seld-initiated.

Comm. for Western Digital.

Seld-initiated.

Sarah Howell

début **art** • Illustrators, Photographers and Fine Artists Agents. 30 Tottenham Street, London, W1T 4RJ. United Kingdom
Tel: 01144 20 7636 1064. Fax: 01144 20 7580 7017. **The Coningsby Gallery** • Tel: 01144 20 7636 7478

email: **info@debutart.com** • **www.debutart.com**

début **art**

Comm. for Virgin Mobile.

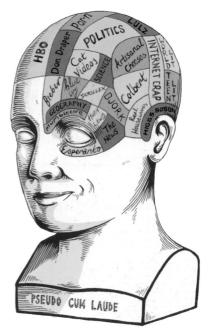

Comm. for Punch Magazine.

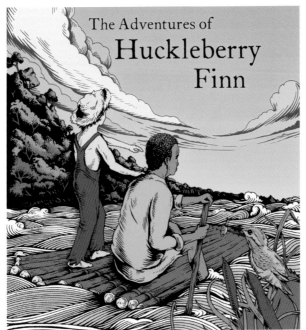

Comm. by Random House Publishing.

Comm. for Infiniti.

⁓e Wilson

⁓but **art** • Illustrators, Photographers and Fine Artists Agents. 30 Tottenham Street, London, W1T 4RJ. United Kingdom
⁓l: 01144 20 7636 1064. Fax: 01144 20 7580 7017. **The Coningsby Gallery** • Tel: 01144 20 7636 7478

⁓nail: **info@debutart.com** • **www.debutart.com**

Comm. by Ted Baker.

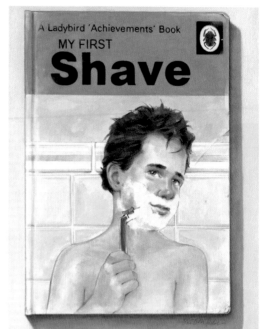

Comm. by Intelligent Life Magazine.

Comm. for Fortnum & Mason.

Comm. for Moët.

Vince McIndoe

début **art** • Illustrators, Photographers and Fine Artists Agents. 30 Tottenham Street, London, W1T 4RJ. United Kingdom
Tel: 01144 20 7636 1064. Fax: 01144 20 7580 7017. **The Coningsby Gallery** • Tel: 01144 20 7636 7478

email: **info@debutart.com** • **www.debutart.com**

Comm. by The Times (UK).

Comm. by McDonald's.

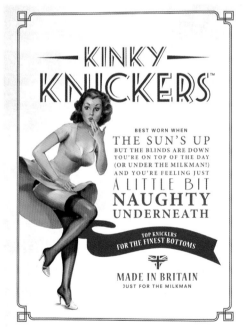

Comm. by Mary Portas.

Comm. for The Ross Poster Group.

Comm. by The Financial Times.

Comm. by The Financial Times.

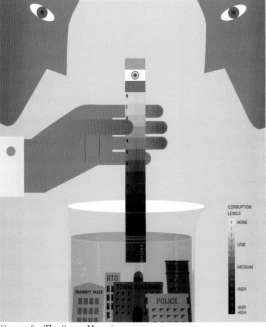

Comm. for The Scene Magazine.

Comm. by Esterson Associates.

Andrew Baker

début **art** • Illustrators, Photographers and Fine Artists Agents. 30 Tottenham Street, London, W1T 4RJ. United Kingdom
Tel: 01144 20 7636 1064. Fax: 01144 20 7580 7017. **The Coningsby Gallery** • Tel: 01144 20 7636 7478

email: **info@debutart.com** • **www.debutart.com**

début art

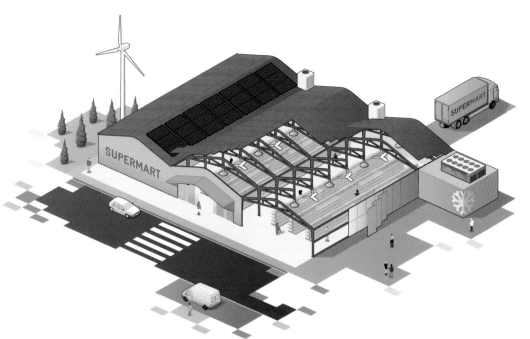

Comm. by Building Magazine.

omm. for BNP Paribas.

Comm. for Invesco.

fomen

but **art** • Illustrators, Photographers and Fine Artists Agents. 30 Tottenham Street, London, W1T 4RJ. United Kingdom
l: 01144 20 7636 1064. Fax: 01144 20 7580 7017. **The Coningsby Gallery** • Tel: 01144 20 7636 7478

ail: **info@debutart.com** • **www.debutart.com**

début **art**

'I Heart Appz'. Self-inititated.

'Out Of The Darkness'. Self-initiated.

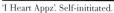

Jacey

début **art** • Illustrators, Photographers and Fine Artists Agents. 30 Tottenham Street, London, W1T 4RJ. United Kingdom
Tel: 01144 20 7636 1064. Fax: 01144 20 7580 7017. **The Coningsby Gallery** • Tel: 01144 20 7636 7478

email: **info@debutart.com** • **www.debutart.com**

'rind'. Self-initiated.

Comm. by Inside Housing Magazine.

Comm. by Men's Health Magazine.

Comm. by The Banker Magazine.

Comm. by BBC Focus Magazine.

Oliver Burston

début **art** • Illustrators, Photographers and Fine Artists Agents. 30 Tottenham Street, London, W1T 4RJ. United Kingdom
Tel: 01144 20 7636 1064. Fax: 01144 20 7580 7017. **The Coningsby Gallery** • Tel: 01144 20 7636 7478

email: **info@debutart.com** • **www.debutart.com**

Comm. by Shortlist Magazine.

Comm. by Bloomberg Businessweek Magazine.

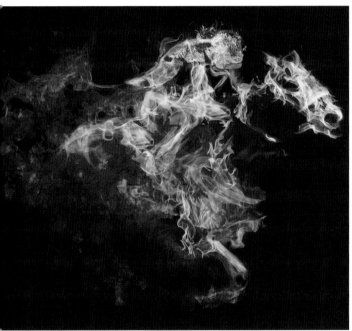

Comm. by WRAP.

Comm. by Futurebrand.

stin Metz

but **art** • Illustrators, Photographers and Fine Artists Agents. 30 Tottenham Street, London, W1T 4RJ. United Kingdom
: 01144 20 7636 1064. Fax: 01144 20 7580 7017. **The Coningsby Gallery** • Tel: 01144 20 7636 7478

ail: **info@debutart.com** • **www.debutart.com**

Jeff Moores

Jmoores1@rochester.rr.com   jeffmoores.com

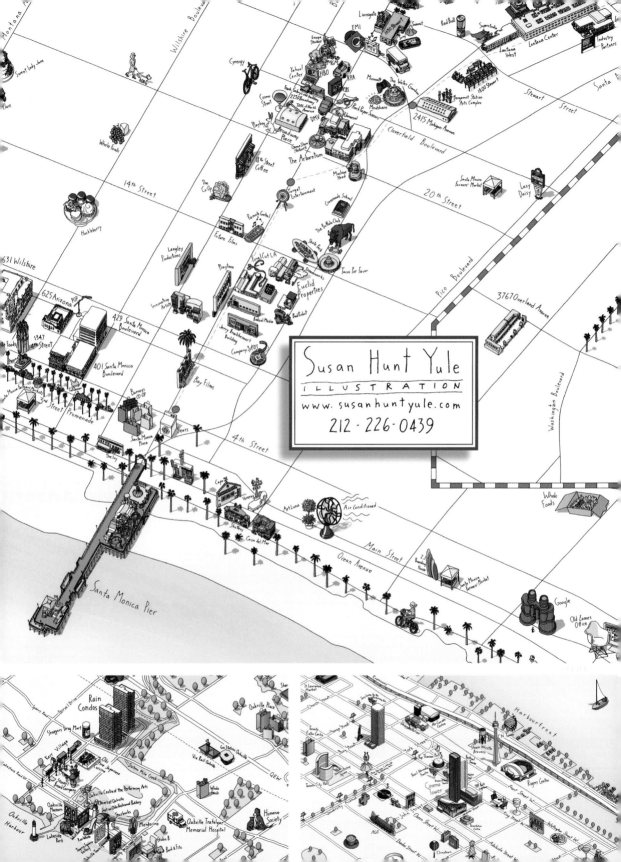

Sassy Cat

Titanic

Dapper Dog

www·pushart·com

meganBerkheiser@pushart.com   mikeCaldwell@pushart.com   212.615.6707

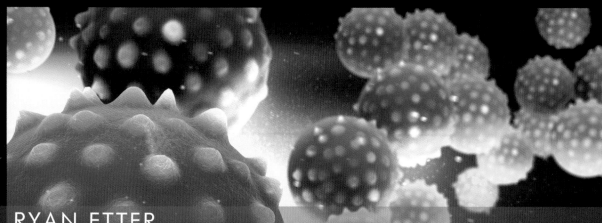

mylestalbot.com

t 011 44 1274 510338   e studio@mylestalbot.com

Michael Pallozzi
47 West 38th St., Suite 1001
New York, NY 10018

mike@pallozzidigital.com
office 212-290-0312
cell 973-769-3743

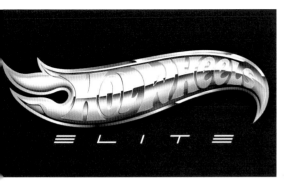

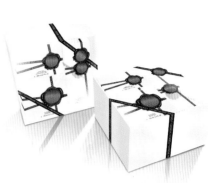

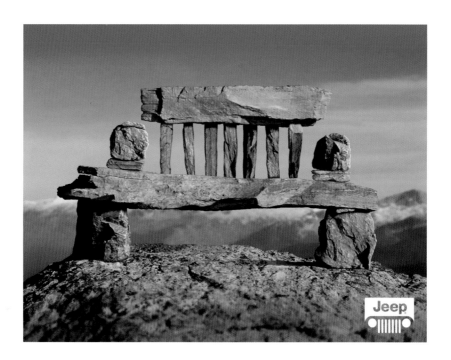

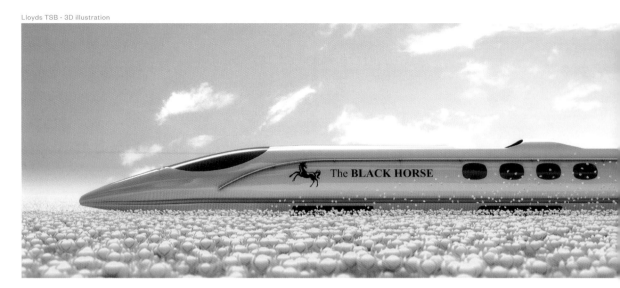

TV advertisement concept illustration

3D Character for SSE

MENDOLA
ARTISTS REPRESENTATIVE

WWW.MENDOLAART.COM

212.986.5680 info@mendolaart.com

HUGH SYME

HUGH SYME

Carluccio's
COLOMBA TRADIZIONALE

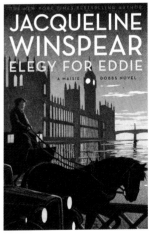

THE NEW YORK TIMES BESTSELLING AUTHOR

JACQUELINE
WINSPEAR
ELEGY FOR EDDIE
A MAISIE DOBBS NOVEL

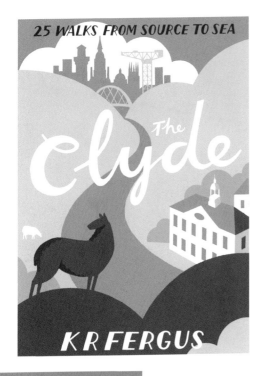

MENDOLA

Matthew Cool

We deliver holiday happiness

The UPS Store

ILLUSTRATION FOR MC DONALD -
AGENCY THE MARKETTING STORE

CAROLINE ATTIA ANIMATION & ILLUSTRATION

_LUSTRATION FOR ETSY TOUCH - IPAD APPLICATION

CANALSAT OVERSEAS- CONTENUS
TV COMMERCIAL - AGENCY : BETC EURORSCG PARIS

Julia Green

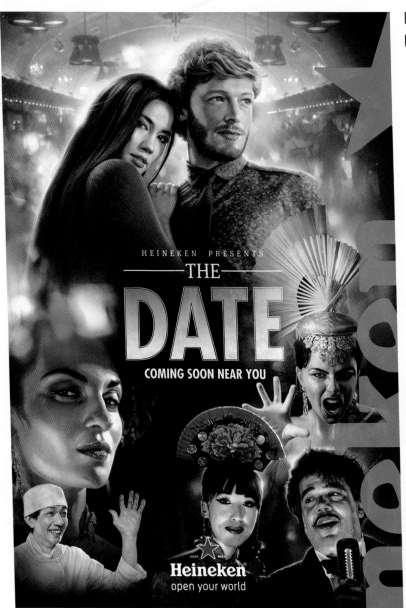

Brendan McCaffrey

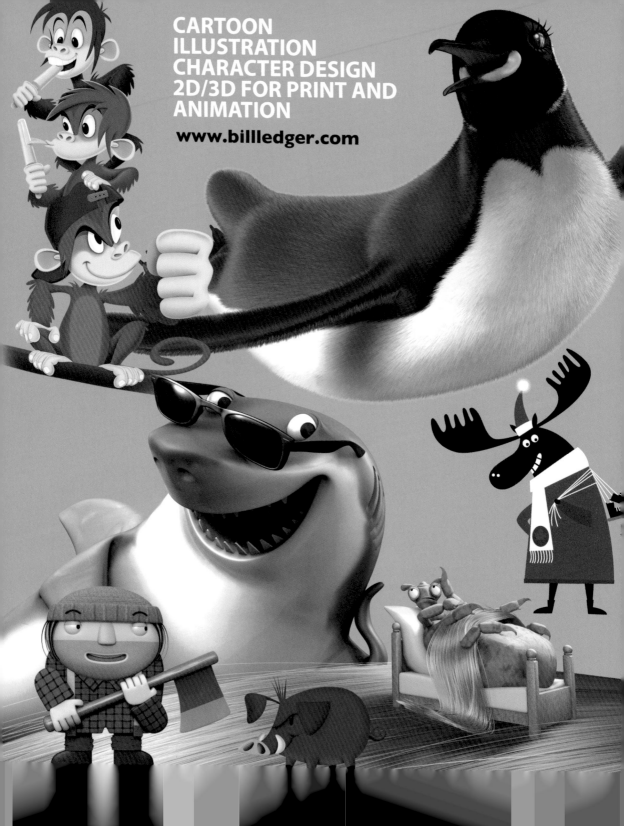

illustration / CGI animation / web

LONDON
YOU ARE HERE!

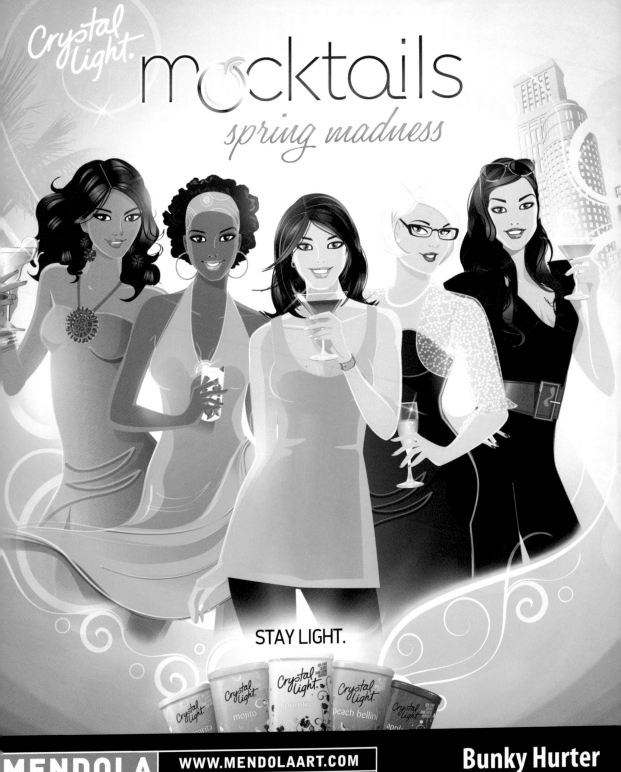

ITE TEA for SMOOTH TASTE

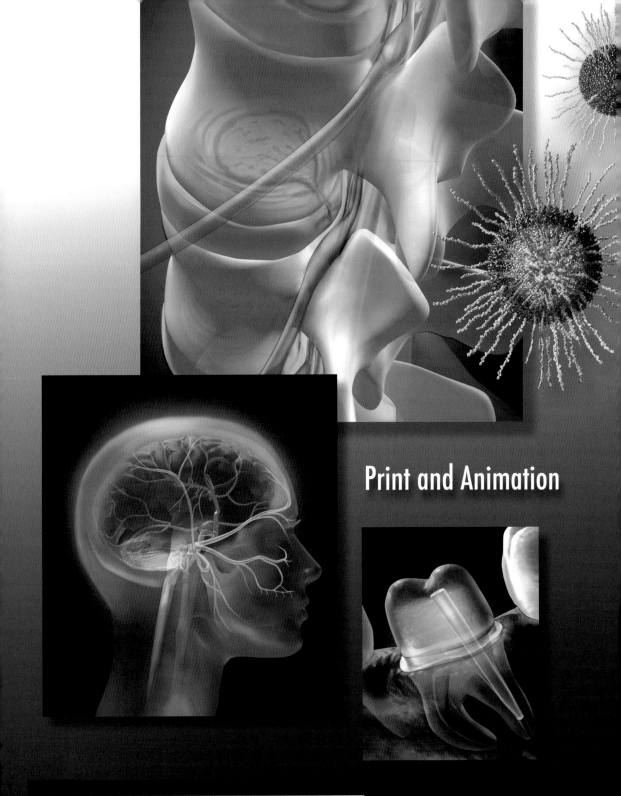

Print and Animation

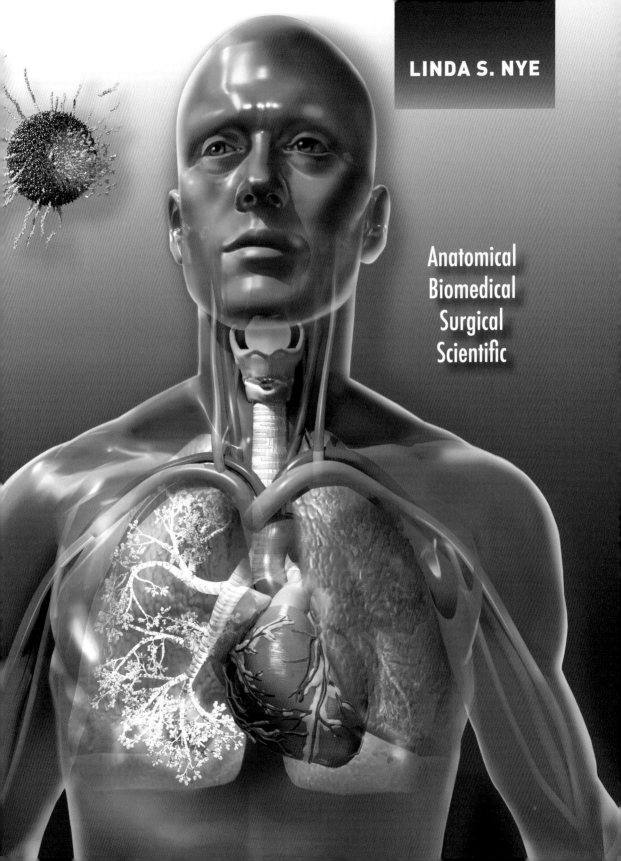

LINDA S. NYE

Anatomical
Biomedical
Surgical
Scientific

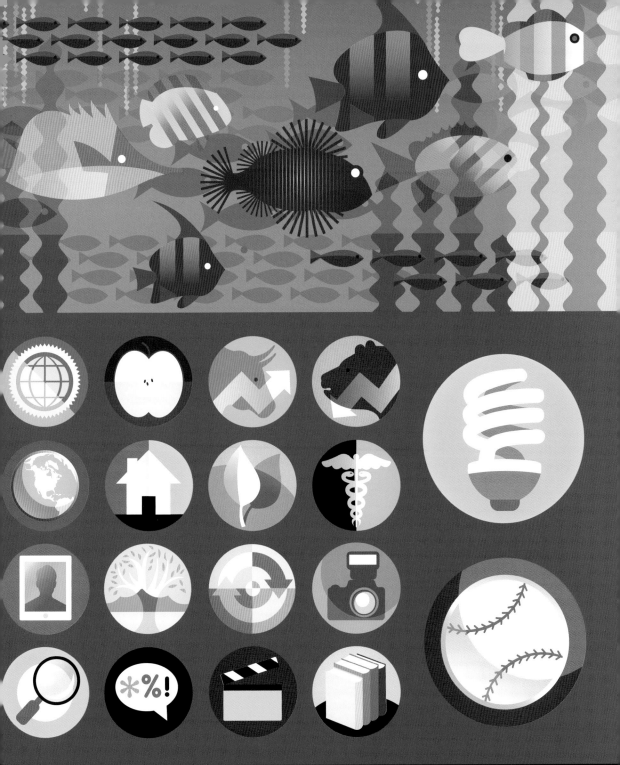

SAM WARD
samwardart.com

MIRACLE ✕ STUDIOS

WEBISODES • MANGA • ONLINE GAMES • COMIC BOOKS • CHARACTER DESIGN • CONCEPT ART

www.miraclestudios.com

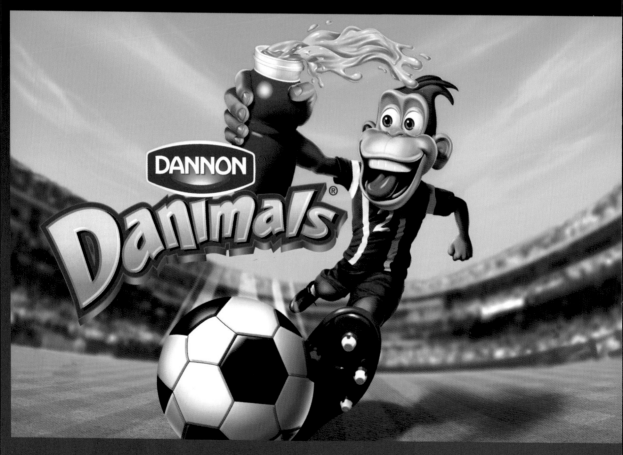

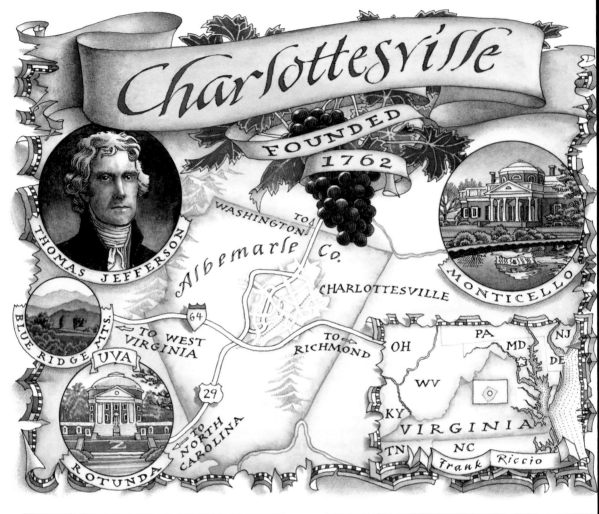

Charlottesville

FOUNDED 1762

THOMAS JEFFERSON

MONTICELLO

BLUE RIDGE MTS.

UVA ROTUNDA

WASHINGTON

Albemarle Co.

CHARLOTTESVILLE

TO WEST VIRGINIA

TO RICHMOND

TO NORTH CAROLINA

64

29

OH

WV

KY

TN

PA

MD

NJ

DE

VIRGINIA

NC

Frank Riccio

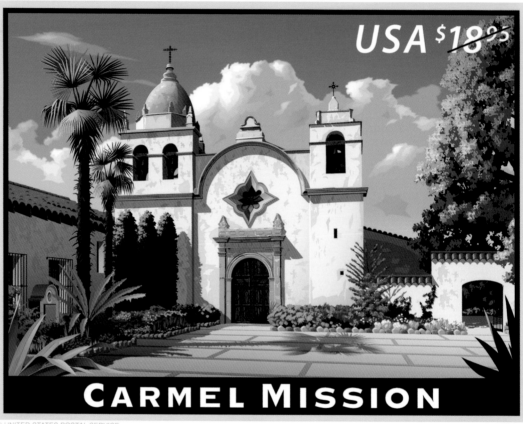

USA $18⁹⁵

CARMEL MISSION

2012

© UNITED STATES POSTAL SERVICE

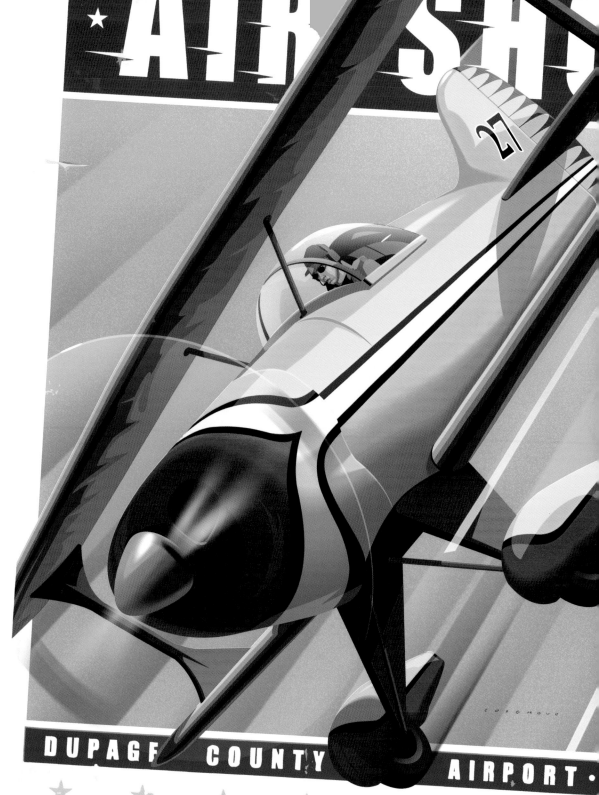

312.765.8911 | cosgrovedesign.com DAN COSGROVE

Blasutta.com | blasuttastudio@aol.com | 631.456.2126

GUY BILLOUT

guy@guybillout.com   www.guybillout.com

Illustration by Judith Drews

RAÚL COLÓN

JOSÉE BISAILLON

ELIZABETH ROSEN

194 THIRD AVE NYC 10003 (212)475-0440
MORGAN GAYNIN INC. MORGANGAYNIN.COM

PATTI MOLLICA

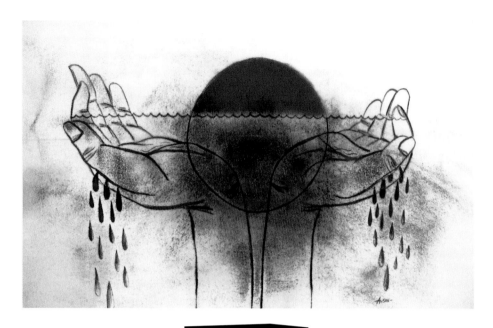

ANSON LIAW

NANETTE BIERS

MORGAN GAYNIN INC

194 THIRD AVE NYC 10003 (212)475-0440

MORGANGAYNIN.COM

A. RICHARD ALLEN

SUSAN GAL

RENÉ MILOT

MY Health and Beauty Regimen

VALERIA PETRONE

CARLO STANGA

194 THIRD AVE NYC 10003 (212)475-0440 MORGANGAYNIN.COM

MORGAN GAYNIN INC

BEPPE GIACOBBE

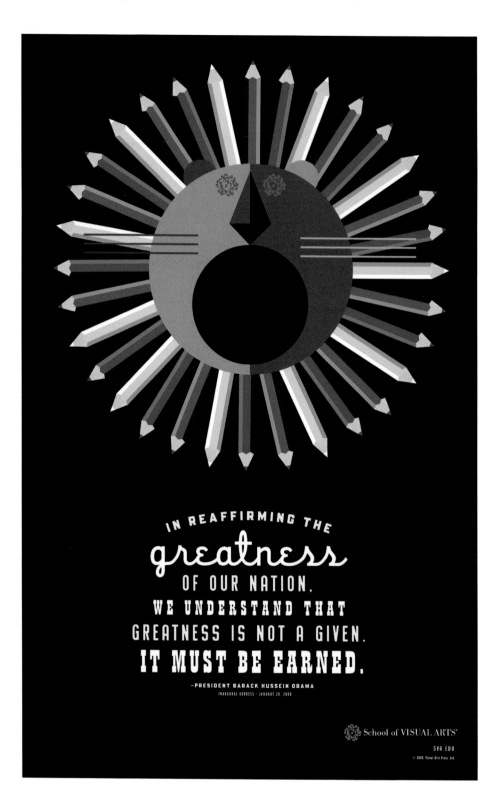